T0194057

Praying *the* Scriptures

*One Woman's Spiritual Mission from
West Africa to Western Europe*

Dr Bummy Ebofin

WESTBOW
PRESS®
A DIVISION OF THOMAS NELSON
& ZONDERVAN

Scripture taken from the King James Version of the Bible.

WestBow Press books may be ordered through booksellers or by contacting:

WestBow Press
A Division of Thomas Nelson & Zondervan
1663 Liberty Drive
Bloomington, IN 47403
www.westbowpress.com
1 (866) 928-1240

ISBN: 978-1-9736-1945-1 (sc)
ISBN: 978-1-9736-1944-4 (hc)
ISBN: 978-1-9736-1946-8 (e)

Library of Congress Control Number: 2018901766

Print information available on the last page.

WestBow Press rev. date: 06/27/2018

DEDICATION

I dedicate this book
in memory of my father, Lekan Ebofin;
my mother, Bukola Ebofin and in appreciation of
the love and support of Fiyin, Fope and Jude

CONTENTS

FOREWORD

Even though written prayers are wonderful, I consider spontaneous prayers the same as communicating with my parents or friends.

Today, I sense the yearning of many to connect more deeply with our heavenly Father and see His kingdom extended. This book is an attempt to stir a passion for His word in every reader and, hopefully, provoke spontaneous, effective and simple heartfelt prayers. I also hope readers can enjoy being in His presence by having productive and easy conversations with Him. I hope that prayers will rise to God from all over the world, bringing renewal and revival in preparation of Jesus' return for His bride – the Church.

My inspiration to write this book came from my experience of attending Christian gatherings led by diverse denominations across Europe, and, particularly, in the United Kingdom. These events were often very successful, although many participants struggled to share prayers spontaneously in public. Prayers were often read collectively but this was sometimes done without thought or enthusiasm. I also observed that prayer meetings were poorly attended, or not too engaging.

If we can cultivate an intimate prayer life, our relationship with Jesus will be transformed. The love of Christ unites us in loving the Father, serving the Son and obeying the Spirit, so we can spread the good news with power, transforming lives and communities. I pray that this truth may be reflected in our attitudes, in our faith adventures and in our prayers as we journey through life together, so that the world may truly believe that we are His disciples.

May this book also spur an ecumenical movement where the Bible, the cross and the name of our Saviour overrides differences in doctrines, Jesus said:

'I pray for them: I pray not for the world, but for them which thou hast given me; for they are thine. And all mine are thine, and thine are mine; and I am glorified in them. And now I am no more in the world, but these are in the world, and I come to thee. Holy Father, keep through thine own name those whom thou hast given me, that they may be one, as we are.' John 17:9-11

All the events in this book are true, but names have been altered to maintain confidentiality. The book gives many scriptural texts as guidance, and as examples in our own contemporary contexts, even though they were originally intended for Jews and later for Gentiles as indicated in the Bible.

PREFACE

I remember walking to church one beautiful Sunday morning, noticing that many were either jogging to keep fit, or with their children preparing for sports activities. I wondered about the challenges faced in raising Christian children keen on sports. Would they have to choose between attending church or participating in sports? Can we promote both spiritual and physical exercise in an increasingly secular world, where attending church is becoming less common? Should we preserve Sundays for worship, and not just for leisure or pleasure activities that exclude God?

I hope this book inspires you to challenge the status quo and spiritually engage with issues significant to you, and to be active rather than passive in promoting godliness in our society. As parents, grandparents and guardians, I pray that we might envision future generations being covered in prayers until Jesus returns. As we prophesy over them, spend time with them, teach them and act as examples, may they experience the joy of loving and serving Christ in the 21st century? They do not need perfect mentors, they simply need authentic ones, willing to share their faith and their weaknesses. Willing to be simple and sincere. Willing to enjoy Him and enjoy life. I pray that our children will encounter the Messiah at an early age, through the reading of scriptures and the fellowship of the saints. May our legacy be to uphold them in righteousness, so their faith can withstand the challenges of their generation? Often they can pass this faith on to their own descendants.

Time and time again, the Israelites were influenced by the spiritual choices of their predecessors. May we share stories, testimonies, celebrations, renewal and revival as we hear and obey the Holy Spirit now and for generations to come? Amen.

ACKNOWLEDGEMENTS

This being my maiden book, I am grateful to God for inspiration as most of it was written within two weeks. However, I am indebted to Sam Cartwright for her time, support and professional skills in editing this book. I am grateful to Roger Van der Steen and Allison Cooper for proofreading. I am thankful for the support, patience and encouragement of my family members; as I submitted my final manuscript the week after my dad's funeral at Lagos, Nigeria.

To God be the glory.

Listen and incline your
Open up your heart to God
Search for peace and silence

Kloster Marinsee

CHAPTER 1

Meditation

He taught me also, and said unto me; let thine heart retain my words: keep my commandments, and live.

Proverbs 4:4

Watching Songs of Praise on TV, I was reminded of my time at Mariensee, a Lutheran women's monastery founded in northern Germany in the thirteenth century. The programme explored ways in which pilgrimages to holy places had impacted peoples' lives. My own brief pilgrimage experience at a 'pop-up, monastery' was enriching, even if the concept was initially confusing.

The pop-up monastery was a 'transient' community of women of various denominations from all over Europe, coming together to pray, share fellowship and live together as an open community.

I had always wanted to experience life in a monastery, and understand how monks and nuns engage with life, work and community, even though I was from a totally different Christian background. How did they discern their calling? How did they deny themselves the comforts of life? Was I disciplined enough to take up this lifestyle? How had an open monastery for women survived for more than eight hundred years? Until 1543, the monastery lived according to the rules of the Cistercians, an order belonging to the Benedictine family. When the Lutheran reformation took place, the women became Protestant. The present house of the monastery was built between 1726-1729. I was intrigued, and realised it would be a once-in-a-lifetime experience for me.

I submitted my application form and was delighted to be accepted. I knew I would be the voice of 'difference', a black dancing and singing Pentecostal lady about to experience very quiet and regimented living! I asked my life group members to pray for me, because I needed a miracle! True to form, God was faithful, because I had one.

I stayed at Mariensee with twenty-eight other women from across Europe and, during this time, I attended a meditation session.

It was not at all what I had expected. I was disappointed because it was led by a theologian and took place in a church. However, the emphasis seemed to be more on t e physical, rather than the spiritual, and spirituality appeared synonymous with nature. There were breathing exercises and silent meditations; I struggled to relate to this approach. We all had our eyes closed, so I started praying under my breath. How long is this for? What else are we expected to do? Was meditation ever mentioned in the Bible? Once I am out of here, I am not coming back for this type of gathering. It was the longest thirty minutes I have ever experienced! I went home to read the Bible and research biblical meditation. In my Bible, I found that meditation was not a new phenomenon, nor was the breathing exercise. Rather, it is an ancient prayer practice endorsed by the Almighty and commended to the Jews in the Old Testament.

As a child I remember reciting and singing Psalm 19:14, 'Let the words of my mouth, and the **meditation** of my heart be acceptable in thy sight, O Lord, my strength and my redeemer'. This meant that meditation was from the heart. So what else does the Bible say about meditation?

> Joshua 1:8 says:
> 'This book of the law shall not depart out of thy mouth; but thou shalt **meditate** therein day and night, that thou mayest observe to do according to all that is written therein: for then thou shalt make thy way prosperous, and then thou shalt have good success.'

Growing up, I read the Bible during my daily quiet times. As a result I could study, ponder, recite, or listen to God speak to me during these times set aside to be with Him. I realised that reading or listening to His word could be likened to eating spiritual food, and meditation could be analogous to digestion; like assimilating nutrients into the bloodstream for the nourishment of the body.

As we meditate, I believe that the revealed scriptural materials gleaned during Bible study feed the mind. The outcome? Revelations, insights, and an increased understanding that feeds the soul, strengthens our faith, and transforms our lives:

> 'For every one that useth milk is unskilful in the word of righteousness: for he is a babe. But strong meat belongeth to them that are of full age, even those who by reason of use have their senses exercised to discern both good and evil.'
> Hebrews 5:13-14

But let's return to my meditation class experience. I was surprised at the absence of scriptures during the session. No biblical texts or biblical lyrics were sung; however, there was silence which I appreciated. During the class we were encouraged to maintain good posture, and we repeatedly performed a series of physical exercises that were demonstrated at the start of the session. Soft music was played from time to time, but there was nothing upon which to meditate!

It was difficult for me to maintain a blank state of mind for a prolonged period. I wondered why it was considered a meditation session? Perhaps a few participants had silently recited God's word, upon which they meditated during the class. Unfortunately, I had come unprepared and assumed that Bibles or Christian songs would be provided.

During my research, I marveled at how the early Christian monks had meditated. Reciting and studying scriptures would have been a common practice at monasteries in former times; however, this art seems to have been lost. As described in Joshua 1:8, when God told Joshua to meditate, it was an *active* and not a passive exercise. Meditation is about actively choosing to listen to Him, so that our spirits can engage with the Holy Spirit to bring forth revelation. We have to find the time to fill the mind with spiritual food for spiritual growth, as encouraged in 1 Peter.

> 'As new born babes, desire the sincere milk of the word, that ye may grow thereby.'
>
> 1 Peter 2:2-3

God's word contains essential nourishment for our spiritual journey. It offers us instruction, guidance, insight, rebuke, encouragement, comfort, and so on. Such inspiration gives us physical, mental and emotional insight, which we can use for inventions, creativity, breakthroughs, wisdom, and also for business, relationship and leadership ideas.

Meditation transforms lives

We are creatures of habit, and reading the Bible is like looking in a mirror; it immediately reveals our shortcomings whenever we are impatient, selfish, uncompromising or proud. The Bible can rebuke us to change for good in a subtle and non-threatening way. Moreover it helps us to tackle difficult issues, and gently encourages us to behave well, in all situations. Eventually this process helps us develop a godly character even though we perpetually fall short of His standard. Looking back to the person I was before I started engaging with the Holy scriptures in meditation, I know my life has been positively influenced.

Meditation could be likened to enjoying private sessions with the Holy Spirit, exchanges that empower and change us. The Bible does not stop there; it reveals divine promises we can all possess:

> 'But foolish and unlearned questions avoid, knowing that they do gender strifes. And the servant of the Lord must not strive; but be gentle unto all men, apt to teach, patient.'
>
> 2 Timothy 2:23-24

Such knowledge, when put into action, pleases our Father even though we still make m stakes. As we develop intimacy with Him, communication becomes easier, much more relaxed, and effective.

Gradually it becomes easier to interact, ask questions, and receive answers. Silence enriches the relationship, since it is the time for listening, and a sign of maturity.

Communicating with God

John Pritchard, in his book entitled, *How Do I Pray?,* mentions that contemplation may start with a verse or image and go on from there. There are no rules, as the main aim is giving attention to God, thereby receiving inspiration and revelation through His words. John Pritchard encourages us to contemplate in silence; however, he likens contemplation to gazing at the face of Jesus. An experience that encourages intimacy in silence, a mature and powerful communicative tool. I think people confuse contemplation with meditation because both can be done in silence, however, contemplation is considered more mystical, whereas meditation is a thought process. Infants are very good at this, communicating by just looking without speaking, dwelling in the present in contentment. What a powerful means of communication: not speaking, but appreciating and acknowledging His presence in our midst.

Reading scriptures during meditation connects our spirits with God, and He whispers to us. God created us in His image, thus we are spirits, we have souls, and we live in human bodies. We therefore connect with Him spiritually.

I can liken hearing Him to tuning in to a walkie-talkie. The airwaves have different frequencies already present in the atmosphere even though they are unseen; we need to pick up the right transmission waves for communication. As we tune in, we connect with various stations, and hear different voices. How do we know we are at the right frequency? How do we link up with the person at the other end whom we cannot see? How do we know it is God speaking? We link up with God spiritually from time to time in the same way that we link up by phone or Skype with friends, listening for a reassuring voice at the other end. His voice is gentle and eager to welcome us into His presence. He is not only our Father but also the creator of the universe, therefore it is respectful to reverence His sovereignty.

In as much as we could not go into a palace and demand to see the monarch without following protocol, we need to respect the Almighty as He is surrounded by angels, elders, and saints. Yet His fatherly nature grants us audience whenever we call on Him. Amazingly, He knows us all by name and yearns for us to have fellowship with Him. He sets aside royal protocol to give us access whenever we call.

Prayer occurs when the Creator and creation communicate. The beauty of meditation is in this silent communion. God not only communicates with humans; He also admires and communicates with all other creatures. That might explain why meditation thrives around nature, especially within a garden or forest setting.

> 'And they heard the voice of the Lord God walking in the garden in the cool of the day: and Adam and his wife hid themselves from the presence of the Lord God amongst the trees of the garden.'
>
> Genesis 3:8

Meditation could be about listening, discerning, silence, guidance, or challenging the status quo. In my case, meditation calms me down as I lay my anxieties to rest with reverence and humility in His presence. One can choose the time, place, and duration, and the Creator will be present there to honour the occasion. The joy is that it can take place anywhere; in the car while driving, while washing up in the kitchen, while in the bathroom, or in the garden. However, it is good to have a habitual time and a special place to be with Him, to hear updates from heaven and know what is on His heart. Prayer is much more than just making a list. Our maturity develops not just by delivering speeches but by listening to Him more, for that is when we obtain wisdom, direction, and breakthrough. 'Truly my soul waiteth upon God: from Him cometh my salvation'. Psalm 62:1

Questions to ponder

- ❖ What benefits have you experienced from meditation?
- ❖ How is Christian meditation different from that of other faiths?
- ❖ Can you take time out to be with God exclusively, or with a prayer partner?

Marinsee, Germany

CHAPTER 2

Call to Prayer

'As the hart (deer), panteth after the water brooks, so panteth my soul after thee, O God. My soul thirsteth for God, for the living God: when shall I come and appear before God?'
Psalm 42: 1-2 (explanation in bracket)

Prayer is a way of communing with God. However, this practice did not take place overnight for me; I had my fair share of struggles when learning to pray.

Why Pray?

I woke up suddenly just after five o'clock in the morning, hearing "Allahu Akbar" ("God is greater" in Arabic). It was my first visit to Kano, the largest city in northern Nigeria, to pursue my internship as a veterinary student for one month. I was staying at a fellow student's house in Kano, though we were both undergraduates of Ibadan University in south west Nigeria.

These early morning Muslim prayers were loud and persistent.

I was a newly born-again Christian and wondered why praying early in the morning was such a big deal. Like most youngsters, I loved my sleep and therefore tried to snooze, but I was restless. I did not have to start work early the next day so I was hoping for a good rest before starting my internship programme with a renowned Veterinary Practice in Kano. I rose reluctantly, as I was unable to go back to sleep, and waited for my hostess to get offer directions to and from the veterinary surgery.

The next day, I woke up before five o'clock, and a voice came to mind - *Why are you not praying, when there is lots to pray about?*

2 Chronicles says:

> 'If my people, which are called by my name, shall humble themselves, and pray, and se k my face, and turn from their wicked ways; then will I hear from heaven, and will forgive their sin, and will heal their land.'
>
> 2 Chronicles 7:14

I was baffled! What should I pray for? How long could I pray? The persistent call to pray very early in the morning went on for days. I could only liken it to God calling Samuel repeatedly until he realised it was God speaking. Samuel was just a child but he had Eli to guide him. This was the summer of 1985, I was in my early twenties and had no one around to advise me. I believe this was my first encounter with the Holy Spirit, who was nudging me to pray. My course mate was not a committed Christian; I knew no one else in Kano. Who could I turn to?

Searching for answers

I went home to Lagos in southern Nigeria after a month in Kano and I was still waking up very early in the mornings. By this time I knew it was a divine call to pray, because each time it happened I was nudged awake, never felt drowsy afterwards and could not go back to sleep. In the mornings, I felt fresh and ready to go about my day, with no knock-on effect from waking up early.

I later returned to my university and came across a book on 'Prayer Mountains', written by Dr David Yonggi Cho, a *South Korean Full Gospel Church* minister. It was about South Koreans waking very early in the mornings to pray for at least an hour. I also read another of his book, *The Fourth Dimension*; which, helped build my faith. I was searching, and longing to know how to pray effectively. It was my first introduction to a life of prayer.

Answering the call

As I continued my faith journey on campus, I regularly attended fellowship with my Christian friends, took on several responsibilities. On 29 March 1986, at a Student Campus Fellowship, held jointly by undergraduates from Lagos, Ibadan, Ife and Ekpoma Universities in Nigeria; I received a public declaration that I was being called into ministry in the presence of hundreds of fellow undergraduates from various universities in south Nigeria. Six of us were called to come up on to the stage, where we were publicly prayed over by other Christians as they set us apart to serve in His kingdom. It reminded me of this scripture:

> 'As they ministered to the Lord, and fasted, the Holy Ghost said, Separate me Barnabas and Saul for the work whereunto I have called them. And when they had fasted and prayed, and laid their hands on them, they sent them away.'
>
> Acts 13:2-3

That was the first and only time I visited Ekpoma University. I believe a revival was moving across Nigeria then, as there was a strong wave of the Holy Spirit among believers. By now I was in my fourth year at veterinary school and many of my lecturers and colleagues thought I would not complete my course, but leave to become an ordained minister due to my passion for Christ. Nevertheless, I completed my degree and remained active in sharing my faith and expressing my love for Him whenever I had the opportunity.

Even though I knew I was called to serve God, I was convinced that I wanted to remain a lay person in kingdom service. During my semester breaks, I travelled to several other university campuses in Nigeria on preaching engagements and to encourage up-and-coming young leaders. While back at my university campus, I frequently met with other Christians and we enjoyed ministering to one another, particularly at weekends, starting on Friday nights. During one such impromptu ministry night at Ibadan University campus, I discerned my ministry. It was not one of the common offices mentioned in 1 Corinthians:

> 'And God hath set some in the church, first apostles, secondarily prophets, thirdly teachers, after that miracles, then gifts of healings, helps, governments, diversities of tongues.'
>
> 1 Corinthians 12:28

Mine was a simple and broad task, and for the first time I realised it was a gift of grace. 'He who exhorts, in exhortation... 'Romans 12:8. I checked the word and it means 'to encourage, to urge, to offer spiritual direction'. To be an encourager and offer spiritual direction were not grand titles for ministry, however I knew that this was my calling. As I continued to read the Bible, I identified several encouragers in the book of Acts. Barnabas was an encourager and so were Pricilla and Aquila. Theirs was an obscure but significant ministry that helped build up other Christians in serving God's people! One had to be grounded in scriptures and shy of the limelight to thrive in this ministry.

'The tidings of these things came unto the ears of the church which was in Jerusalem: and they sent for Barnabas, that he should go as far as Antioch. Who, when he came, and had seen the grace of God, was glad, and exhorted them all, that with purpose of heart they would cleave unto the Lord. For he was a good man, full of the Holy Ghost and of faith: and much people was add d unto the Lord. Then departed Barnabas to Tarsus, for to seek Saul.

> 'After these things Paul departed from Athens, and came to Corinth; And found a certain Jew named Aquila, born in Pontus, lately come from Italy, with his wife Priscilla; (because that Claudius had commanded all Jews to depart from Rome:) and came unto them. And because he was of the same craft, he abode with them, and wrought: for by their occupation they were tentmakers'
>
> Acts 11:22-25,

> 'And Paul after this tarried there yet a good while, and then took his leave of the brethren, and sailed thence into Syria, and with him Pricilla and Aquila: having shorn his head in Cenchrea (in Greece).'
>
> Acts 18:18

> 'And a certain Jew named Apollos, born at Alexandria, an eloquent man, and mighty in the scriptures, came to Ephesus. This man was instructed in the way of the Lord; and

being fervent in the spirit, he spake and taught diligently the things of the Lord, knowing only the baptism of John. And he began to speak boldly in the synagogue: whom when Aquila and Priscilla had heard, they took him unto them, and expounded unto him the way of God more perfectly.'

Acts 18:24-26

I prayed at that time that God would give me opportunities to serve and encourage fellow Christians wherever I was in the world. Little did I know where I would end up.

Questions to ponder

- ❖ What is God calling you to do?
- ❖ How do you discern your call?
- ❖ Is there anyone you can mentor, or can someone assist you with your faith walk?

CHAPTER 3

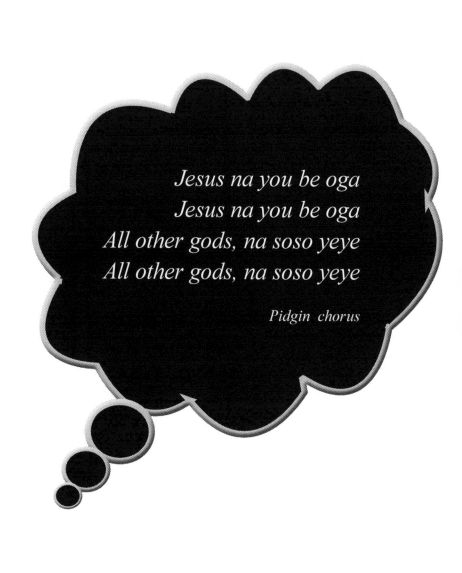

Praying with Scriptures

'For the word of God is quick, and powerful, and sharper than any two-edged sword, piercing even to the dividing asunder of soul and spirit, and of the joints and marrow, and is a discerner of the thoughts and intents of the heart.'

Hebrews 4:12

One of my favourite phrases in life is: 'work smarter, not harder'. Why reinvent the wheel when you can use existing resources more efficiently to achieve the same goals? I consider the Bible a book of effective prayers, as does the Psalmist: 'The words of the Lord are pure words: as silver tried in a furnace of earth, purified seven times'. Psalm 12:6

I liken studying scriptures to treasure hunting! Where are the gems buried? How do I locate them for future use? I know I am not great at reciting from memory, therefore I use bookmarks during study for easy identification or referencing of appropriate verses in times of need. Proverbs 7 says:

> 'My son, keep my words, and lay up my commandments within thee.'
>
> Proverbs 7:1

I was in Malawi a few years ago, attending an African leadership conference organised by the Malawi Bible Society. I was blown away by the youngsters' dedication to memorising chapters of scriptures; the whole of 2Thessalonians, all five chapters of the book of James, the long chapters of Isaiah 54 and 60! I was immensely impressed. How wonderful and glorious to be filled with the Holy scriptures! I remember teaching my children to memorise scriptures when they were very young, but they were short Psalms and memory verses, not as impressive as I had see in Malawi. My best shot in terms of teaching chapters of scriptures was to teach my son at the early age of four to memorise and recite Psalm 20 (my favourite psalm) on the platform at church, when I was his Sunday school teacher. I might have been influenced by the fact that I know Muslim children memorise and recite the Quran when they are young, so that it is not easy to dislodge their faith when they become adults. They must have learnt this principle from Jews reciting the Torah, and Christians reciting the Bible.

As a young mother, I taught my children scriptures in snippets by encouraging them to recite memory verses on a weekly basis, especially on Fridays which was their 'sweetie day'. Often my daughter outperformed my son because she loved the challenge, but my son loved the reward! In the end, it was fun to read, sing and recite scriptures together. Even though they had different personalities, the end result was to keep His commands in our hearts so they could bear good fruits and help to please Him.

Along the way, I discovered that it was easier for children and youths to remember scriptures using songs, or linking scriptures with play, drama, puppet shows and hand actions. As a Sunday school teacher and Bible club leader at that time, I also had to recite and remember the memory verses week after week, to remind or correct my students. I understood their challenges and wondered who was struggling more to remember? Together we had fun and we laid a good foundation for the future, particularly when recalling memory verses in times of trials.

Scriptural prayers

Praying publicly is not an easy feat and, in the African context, one is expected to pray spontaneously from the heart when called upon, whenever and wherever. Highlighted texts or Bible bookmarks come in handy during corporate or public prayers. I find it helpful to base the prayers around scriptural texts, reading out the texts and changing the emphasis and tone to reflect the occasion. Scriptures sometimes sound poetic, especially during thanksgiving and adoration, and we are glad when the passage reflects the mood of the event. For example, rejoicing with those who rejoice, and mourning with those who mourn.

I love reading verses from the Song of Solomon in wedding contexts because they seem very appropriate, and right for the occasion. On the other hand, there are Psalms for bereavement, feeling abandoned, rejected, and lonely or in despair. If one is not use to praying aloud in public, it is advisable to prepare the texts ahead of time, and it doesn't matter if the prayers are short. Just read out appropriate scriptures and, if possible, change statements into requests, based on Bible promises to suit the occasion. These prayers are potent, since they come directly from scriptures; God honours your trust in His word:

'I will worship toward thy holy temple, and praise thy name for thy loving kindness and for thy truth: for thou hast magnified thy word above all thy name.'

Psalm 138:2

This passage affirms that God honours scriptures presented in prayer, because His word is His bond! What a wonderful promise! Even though we may have read the Bible daily for years, it never loses its power, mystery or inspiration.

In life, we have fast, voracious readers and s ow drip-feeders. Many people are able to read the whole Bible in a year and other slowcoaches like me take years to get through the whole Bible! Whichever camp you are in, what we accrue from reading and meditating on the words is what matters.

I remember visiting the En Gedi area in Israel a few years ago, just walking distance from the Dead Sea. When I visited the botanical garden near En Gedi, I appreciated the significance of drip-feeding. I looked to my right and saw the most beautiful botanical landscape with lots of beautiful shrubs, trees and flowering plants. When I looked in the opposite direction, it was pure desert, with nothing but sand. What a contrast, how could this be? There were man-made lakes and reservoirs for watering the dry land using networks of water pipes. The large pipes transporting water from reservoirs were connected to smaller water pipes forming a spaghetti of small thin hoses, continuously drip-feeding each plant in the botanic garden with drops of water. After soaking the land with water, ensuring appropriate nutrients were present and planting the right seeds or seedlings, the plants flourished. The conglomeration of the different plants became a garden, where communities thrived, in sharp contrast to the rest of the arid landscape.

For me, this was a demonstration of how the water of life from our Holy scriptures can soak our lives continuously, bringing life and beauty to arid situations, as we stay connected to the source through Jesus. Communing regularly with God yields fruitfulness in our Christian walk, even though we stumble from time to time. In addition, consistent quiet times encourage regular one-to-one meetings with our Father, promote discussions with our Saviour and stimulate divine appointments by the Holy Spirit. These are exclusive sessions to be guarded in our diaries. As we commune regularly with God, we imbibe His nature with the hope that the interaction transforms us. The good thing is that these appointments are not formal and we are free to alter the agenda as it suits. Our meetings are confidential and only our angels in addition to the Trinity are present, unless family and friends are invited along.

It is best to listen more and speak less, and fortunately, we can rebook our appointments as often as we wish. Bill Hybels said in his book *Simplify*, that the best way to simplify life is by efficient diary management. We should allot times for the more important life issues first, and then work around them to avoid prioritising the urgent above the important. Another great thing about spending time with the Holy Spirit is that our fellowship with Him can reflect in our mood. For example, we can select celebratory psalms reflecting praise, thanksgiving and worship. Or we can express despondency, sadness and concerns with appropriate scriptures as the psalmist did. During worship and Bible study we may also receive revelation, direction or solutions. In addition to worship, Bible study progresses with the use of various bible resources such as commentaries or internet talks to develop bespoke plans that complement visual, audio or manual learning styles. For example, a friend recently told me how Christians in South Korea write out passages of scriptures during bible study. These are compiled and the hand-written manuscripts are passed on as gifts to their children or relatives. This is an example of adopting a manual learning style, and the scripts become assets! Auditory learners often listen to an audio Bible, recorded sermons and messages, or Christian songs containing scriptural truths. Visual learners could use printed resources or online videos. These different learning styles make Bible study fun, increase knowledge and strengthen faith.

New outlook

I was introduced to corporate prayers in a fun way. Though newly born again on campus, I still wanted to enjoy my undergraduate life. I had fallen in love with my Saviour, however, being young, I did not want to miss out on youthful activities. For example, most campus parties took place on Friday and Saturday nights except during exam periods. There were lots of young men with cars parked outside the female student accommodation at weekends hoping to take girls out to various social events. Weekend parties were great for dancing and networking with acquaintances, since we worked very hard on our professional courses during the week.

Freshers week was fun, new students were often the center of attraction and in high demand for social outings. I was the President of the only all-female club on campus – the Feminic club in my second year, so I was quite well-connected. Members of the Feminic club were mostly undergraduates enrolled on professional courses such as medicine, pharmacy, engineering, etc. and the focus was to help the disadvantaged and marginalised in society. The club ran many fundraising activities, and provided a welcome break from our studies. We organised activities such as fashion shows and car wash sessions to raise awareness of the plight of disabled children and orphans in our community We visited several orphanages especially Cheshire Home in Ibadan, and I found the work rewarding.

Despite the good works, I was not yet a fully committed Christian. I was studious, with good grades and good morals, and the Feminic club activities made me popular on campus. However, I was not content with life, as I had not completely surrendered my life to Jesus. I was still struggling with transitioning from 'fun girl' to a 'church girl'. None of my close friends in the Feminic club was a born again Christian, and I wondered whether the two things were compatible. How should I manage my new identity? Many of the campus Christians forbade parties and alcohol. I could live without alcohol, but I missed my social outings and did not see how to negotiate both lifestyles. When I enquired, I was told:

> 'Therefore, if any man be in Christ, he is a new creature: old things are passed away; behold, all things are become new'.
>
> 2 Corinthians 5:17

My lifestyle had to change, but I was not convinced. Being outspoken, I told God how much I loved Him, and explained that I was not ready for a boring lifestyle as a Christian. After much discussion with Him in my heart, I eventually reached a turning point. I attended a party one weekend. It was quite late at night, and most parties in those days took place at social halls or at a friend's home. With my new identity, I was quiet and reserved; friends came and asked if I had truly joined the Scripture Union? When I confirmed that I had, they asked what I was doing at the party. I avoided answering this question as I did not know the answer myself. The atmosphere was loud and smoky, which made me uncomfortable for the first time. Strangely, I became more sensitive to the language being used around me, and sensed that something deep within me had changed. I did not belong here! I had less in common with these acquaintances and felt lonely, despite the busy and noisy atmosphere.

All of a sudden, one of my favourite tunes was being played: Red, Red Wine by UB40. I pleaded with my Heavenly Father to allow me to dance to this piece of music, and told him that afterwards I would obey and follow Him wholeheartedly. I got up and danced to the best of my ability, my countenance brightened and my old self resurfaced. All my friends were surprised and glad to see me so cheerful. We sang loudly together and later I said my goodbyes and left, realising that I had changed for good. I knew I belonged elsewhere, and indeed I was a new person!

That evening was a turning point for me. I do not believe that parties are sinful; even Christ attended celebrations. However, it is important to choose close friends who are aware of and interested in our new spirituality. Sometimes we need to be bold, and gently end friendships that do not support and encourage our new identity as a disciple of Christ. However, this is a decision only you can make. Listen to God's prompting, and choose carefully.

As I fast-forward to recent years, the reality of such truths still holds. Recently, my twenty-five-year-old son went out with friends, all postgraduate students seeking some relaxation on a Friday night. Unbeknown to them, the drink of one friend was 'spiked'. When they realised that one of them was badly affected, the whole group left. As a group of trustworthy friends, they were divinely protected on that occasion; however, we are more vulnerable when outside the safety net of Christians, close friends or responsible people.

This made me think back and realise that God was very gentle and understanding with me as a youth. He did not lay down legalistic rules, but gave me options with consequences. I realise now that as an immature Christian, the friends we make and the actions we take influence our faith walk. Good Christian friends support great choices, which help us grow; bad friends may cause us to lose our faith. Especially if they have strong personalities that disregard our own preferences. Choose wisely.

Corporate prayers

Going back to my undergraduate life as a young believer, after the last party experience, I had to figure out how to spend my Friday evenings. As new and eager young disciples, we started meeting in one of our rooms on campus. Before we knew it, ten to twelve of us were coming together regularly. Slowly we started praying for one another. We raised urgent, important, mundane and silent prayer requests and shared issues affecting our studies, homes and communities, gradually including intercessory prayer for national and global challenges. We also shared revelations, testimonies and learnt new Christian songs. We played Christian tunes, danced, sang, made melodies to God, replaced the words of popular melodies with Christian lyrics. We enjoyed being youths as well as serving God. Little did we know that we were fulfilling the instructions in the book of Colossians:

> 'Let the word of Christ dwell in you richly in all wisdom; teaching and admonishing one another in psalms and hymns and spiritual songs, singing with grace in your hearts to the Lord. And whatsoever ye do in word or deed, do all in the name of the Lord Jesus, giving thanks to God the Father by Him.'
>
> Colossians 3:16-17

By the time Sunday came, we were on fire! We came to the Sunday meeting charged. We continued reading scriptures, praising God, and prophesying. God moved among us because we were hungry, yearning for Him and seeking to know Him. This led to my first experience of the move of the Holy Spirit.

Exciting prayer meetings

> 'Then said Jesus unto the twelve, 'Will ye also go
> away?' Then Simon Peter answered him, 'Lord,
> to whom shall we go?' Thou hast the words of
> eternal life. And we believe and are sure that you
> are Christ, the Son of the living God.'
>
> John 6:67-69

After a few years of campus fellowship, most of my Christian friends graduated, and new, younger Christians took up leadership roles in our fellowship. I was in my final year of Veterinary Medicine, which was a five year degree course, so I decided to start attending an independent Charismatic church, off campus. The great thing about our campus fellowship was that it was ecumenical, and belonged to no single denomination. We followed instructions from the Bible and appointed leaders according to our gifts. I often hear people say that these kinds of groups might misinterpret the Bible. My response is, if you genuinely seek God, you will find Him! His Spirit will lead you into all truth and show you the way to go. After all, the Great Commission commands us to go, and He shall be with us always!

Christian life on campus was great, because we did not have to adhere to church traditions that sometimes stifled the outworking of the scriptures as they did in the days of the Pharisees and Sadducees? Little did I know that I was preparing for future life off campus at Scripture Pasture Church, led by Pastor Olubi, who was a university lecturer.

'Scripture Pasture' was exciting and I became a member straight away. The church comprised mostly of Ibadan University students and a few lecturers. There was an interesting church culture in this community. If a person was interested in becoming a church member, they were assigned to join the prayer team for the first three months. This placement had several functions: to help new members learn how to pray, and to help them discern their ministry within the community. Effective prayer was the gateway through which we launched our ministries within and without the church; this was where my prayer skills advanced. The prayer team met an hour before services on a Sunday and every Friday was a prayer and fasting day for all church workers, culminating in a two-hour prayer session between six and eight o'clock on Friday evenings. What did we pray for? How did we pray? I learnt there and then that the secrets of an exciting prayer meeting were preparation, expectation and discipline.

We were given a list of prayer points. To enhance prayer times, I found researching scriptures beforehand helped anchor prayers and boost faith. We came with expectation, adoration and thanksgiving to bless God and thank Him for His faithfulness. We were disciplined enough to allocate sufficient time, and to allow for spontaneous requests as led by the Holy Spirit. From time to time we were encouraged to remain silent to listen to God, and to create space for ministry and divine visitation.

Towards the end of the prayer time we would have a period of rest and refreshment because our souls had travailed in prayers, which could be likened to a spiritual workout.

It took a lot of discipline not to break the fast, and many drank water during the day to stay hydrated. When we managed to stand firm and complete the fast, we felt strengthened within. We shared scriptures together, sang a song and went home to break the fast.

Here are some examples of power scriptures that declared our position in Christ in God:

> 'Blessed be the God and Father of our Lord Jesus Christ, who hath blessed us with all spiritual blessings in heavenly places in Christ: According as he hath chosen us in him before the

foundation of the world, that we should be holy and without blame before him in love. Having predestinated us unto the adoption of children by Jesus Christ to himself, according to the good pleasure of his will, To the praise of the glory of his grace, wherein he hath made us accepted in the beloved'

Ephesians 1:3-6

'For this cause we also, since the day we heard it, do not cease to pray for you, and to desire that ye might be filled with the knowledge of his will in all wisdom and spiritual understanding; that ye might walk worthy of the Lord unto all pleasing, being fruitful in every good work, and increasing in the knowledge of God; strengthened with all might, according to his glorious power, unto all patience and longsuffering with joyfulness; giving thanks unto the Father, which hath made us meet to be partakers of the inheritance of the saints in light: who hath delivered us from the power of darkness, and hath translated us into the kingdom of his dear Son.'

Colossians1:9-13

By the end of the prayer meeting, we were assured in our spirits, and I experienced peace within, knowing that we had touched God, and that God had touched us too. As intercessors, our highest desire was to develop such a close relationship with God that He would disclose His plans and secrets with us, as He did with Father Abraham in Genesis 18.

Ecumenical forums

My early Christian experience on campus prepared me well for the real world. I did not know where I was going to live, work or attend church, however, I knew that wherever I ended up living I was going to look for a church where Christ's supremacy was celebrated and the Holy Spirit was free to operate. In Nigeria, I attended charismatic churches and then I found myself in the UK.

It was easy for me to settle at the Elim Pentecostal Church in Belfast because that was the specific church to which I was sent to serve. However, when I moved to England, the story was different. God certainly had a good sense of humour and He still sends His angels to stir the waters and uphold unity in diversity.

Since moving to England, I have attended many ecumenical forums. I was first introduced to these ecumenical groups when I started work at the Church Mission Society (CMS) in London. CMS later moved to an office in Oxford which was located very near Blackbird Leys estate, one of the largest housing estates in the country. As an evangelical, I was interested in witnessing and networking within this community near my office. Various church representatives met together to pray and seek ways of working together to spread the gospel within this very large community, which had a mixed reputation in the area. Joining the ecumenical group was useful as I was new to Oxford city, although I was concerned about these ecumenical prayer meetings which were to be conducted by different churches with various styles. Would it be hit and miss? Would it be exciting or boring? How would we pray together?

A prayer meeting says a lot about a church or organization; it is a good indicator of its spirituality. Prayer is the engine that drives the church and connects it to the source. If the church loses its ability to pray, it loses its ability to hear from God and to do His will on earth as it is in heaven. As Jesus said, quoting Isaiah

6:7 in Mark 11:17, 'Is it not written, My house shall be called of all nations the house of prayer?'

On various occasions we discussed the practicality of working together to serve the Blackbird Leys community. However, there was a lack of spiritual engagement, because the Church is increasingly better at organising activities than hearing from God. At many of the ecumenical forums I attended, prayers were said using books of prayers but I noted that spending time on scriptures to discern and understand His will occurred less often.

How can we be a house of prayer for all nations when we cannot pray effectively? Why has prayer become so dull and relegated to only the start and end of events? Has prayer become a side issue rather than the core of all activities? If we are the bride of Christ, why is it so difficult to commune with our bridegroom, Jesus? What does the church offer the world if it cannot pray effectively and speak the mind of God with authority and power? Why do we increasingly excel in the mundane above the spiritual?

In the end, I joined the Community Church at Blackbird Leys to get to know the residents better and engage with its issues spiritually. By God's grace, I was able to conduct half a night of prayer several times by staying with a friend on the estate. I also stayed late at work one day a week to attend a house group at Blackbird Leys, and get to know the residents. There were breakthroughs and the Community Church was doing an amazing job.

Ecumenical meeting in Germany

After attending another ecumenical forum, this time in Europe, I realised that the problems I had observed were not restricted to the UK. Europe is becoming increasingly secular, and its hope and future lies in prayer for spiritual breakthrough.

Christian women from twenty-eight countries gathered together for a week, desperate to make a prayerful difference on the continent. Where were we to start? We managed to overcome our language barriers, but struggled with spontaneous prayers from the heart. Then I began to realise that even though we were from different denominations, we had several things in common: belief in the Trinity, belief in Christ as our Saviour, recognition that the Bible is God's word, acknowledgement of the power of prayer and a desire to seek peace and justice for the poor. Therefore we could all pray to the Father, through His Son, using the scriptures. When I was asked to lead a short night vigil we prayed for salvation, a move of God, and peace and justice for the continent.

I realised that this approach could work anywhere, and in any country. God is the same everywhere. We all joined together in praying this text:

> 'O Lord, God of heaven, the great and terrible God, that keepeth covenant and mercy for them that love him and observe His commandments. Let thine ears now be attentive and thine eyes open, that thou mayest hear the prayer of Thy servant, which I pray before thee now, day and night, for the children of Israel thy servants, and confess the sins of the children of Israel, which we have sinned against thee: both I and my father's house have sinned. We have dealt very corruptly against thee, and have not kept the commandments, nor the statutes, nor the judgements, which thou commandest thy servant Moses.'
>
> Nehemiah 1: 5-7

While confessing these verses as a prayer, I encouraged

the participants at the vigil to swap "Israelites" for their own nationality, so as to personalise the prayer and make it relevant. The opportunity to use scripture as a prayer tool, particularly where doctrines and language differed, worked well. After open prayer times, people smiled, came together and praised His name. Praying scriptures helps members of an ecumenical group to focus. Praying scriptures transforms individuals, churches, communities and nations by exalting Christ over doctrines and traditions. As we celebrate our diverse traditions at corporate events, we can apply this simple and effective approach, because it works! I invite you to give it a try.

Questions to ponder

- ❖ How much time can I spend in searching scriptures?
- ❖ Could it help me pray more specifically and effectively?
- ❖ Do I come to meetings prepared and expectant?

Ijinga - Tanzania

CHAPTER 4

Thanksgiving

O come, let us sing unto the Lord: let us make a joyful noise to the rock of our salvation. Let us come before His presence with thanksgiving, and make a joyful noise unto Him with psalms.

Psalm 95:1-2

In 2005, I celebrated my fortieth birthday and my whole family travelled to the United States. During the weekend, on Easter Sunday to be precise, we visited the Redeemed Christian Church of God based in Maryland. It was a majority black church and its members were mostly Nigerians with more than 1,000 people in attendance at the service. As many people know, Africans are in no hurry in God's presence. During the service there were lots of testimonies, songs and celebrations with dancing. After the testimonies, it was time for a special Easter thanksgiving. The minister announced that worship and thanksgiving would be conducted in the traditional way. I wondered what that meant. It was our first time in the church, and to my surprise, everyone either prostrated themselves or knelt before God! The church floor was carpeted and both young and old, male and female, guests and members bowed down before God, recounting His blessings upon their lives and thanking God for His mercies and provisions. It was mass worship but privately executed. We all spoke individually to God, disregarding the people around us. This was our special time with God and we did not wish to waste time looking around or checking what our neighbour was doing in case God passed us by! We praised God, magnified Him, earnestly spoke about our lives, as if we were having a private audience with God. We laid all bare before Him, not caring what anyone thought of us; nor did we check how much time we spent – this was our personal appointment with Him. Why come to church if you have no serious business with God?

As we stood in the presence of our resurrected Redeemer, who is constantly praying for us and pleading our cause before the throne of grace, it was an extraordinary service. We did not have to book an appointment or pay legal fees to meet with Him. Why would we not be eager to engage with our advocate who is able to advise us, support us and win our case?

It was time to worship Him without restraint; to forfeit my reputation by bowing before Him and declaring His greatness as I laid face down in His presence. I was so proud to be a Christian, and a follower of Christ. I was glad for His love for me and my family. That day, I experienced what it meant to exalt God in spirit and in truth, regardless of my surroundings. I was lost in His presence. I felt like Mary Magdalene waiting in the garden, not knowing what to expect, but sensing that her Lord might be near. I remembered that Mary's expectations were realised, when she saw Jesus on His way to heaven to present His resurrected, pierced body to God the Father as the accepted sacrifice for sin! The gospel of John recorded the brief discussion Jesus had with Mary at the garden tomb that early Easter morning.

> 'And seeth two angels in white sitting, the one
> at the head, and the other at the feet, where

the body of Jesus had lain. And they say unto her, 'Woman, why weepest thou?' She saith unto them, 'Because they have taken away my Lord, and I know not where they have laid him'. And when she had thus said, she turned herself back, and saw Jesus standing, and knew not that it was Jesus. Jesus saith unto her, 'Woman, why weepest thou?' 'Whom seekest thou?' She, supposing him to be the gardener, saith unto him, 'Sir, if thou have borne him hence, tell me where thou hast laid him, and I will take him away.' Jesus saith unto her, 'Mary'. She turned herself, and saith unto him, 'Rabboni'; which is to say, Master. Jesus saith unto her, 'Touch me not'; for I am not yet ascended to my Father: but go to my brethren, and say unto them, I ascend unto my Father, and your Father; and to my God, and your God'. Mary Magdalene came and told the disciples that she had seen the Lord, and that He had spoken these things unto her.'

John 20: 13-18

After a considerable time, we all stood up, rejoiced, listened to the sermon and continued the Easter celebrations with friends. It was so special! We could sense God's anointing to heal, to save and to deliver! God obviously could not resist the adoration pouring out from His people, and He drew near as we expressed gratitude for what He had done in our lives, and worshipped Him. What a glorious thanksgiving service.

Celebrate the marriage supper

Christianity is a lot of fun. On various occasions I have seen and heard Christian Comedians present clean, funny jokes.

Whenever I get the opportunity to lead or share among friends, I tell them jokingly that there will be division of labour in heaven, when celebrating the marriage supper of the bridegroom and his bride, the Church:

> 'Let us be glad and rejoice, and give honour to Him: for the marriage of the Lamb is come, and his wife hath made herself ready. And to her was granted that she should be arrayed in fine linen, clean and white: for the fine linen is the righteousness of saints. And he said to me, 'Write, blessed are they which are called unto the marriage supper of the Lamb'. And He said unto me, these are the true sayings of God.'
>
> Revelation 19:7-9

If God ever asked for my opinion on this matter, I would suggest that Europeans organise the ceremony to ensure that we arrive promptly and have a great order of service. The North Americans would handle security to prevent any gatecrashing. South Americans would be responsible for the processions and carnival, as we parade in different tribes and tongues singing and making melody to the Trinity. The Middle Eastern, Asian and Pacific people groups would be responsible for food – we could have a range of delicious and very healthy options. The Australians, and New Zealanders would make the barbecues – with seafood from the river flowing beneath the throne of grace. And yes, you guessed it; the Africans and West Indians would be in charge of praise, worship and dancing! Psalm 150 would come alive. Praising with drums, steel bands, cymbals – making music for all as we worship the King of kings and Lord of lords. Jehovah would be present, and the gentle, dynamic and powerful Holy Spirit. Angels and elders would be watching on and joining us in worship, whilst the demons might wish to gatecrash but would be unable to. The early saints would lead the celebration and we would join them in jubilation. What a great occasion it will be. Heaven will be fun, so we need to start practicing here and now.

Worship

Worship is about pleasing God, not us. Preaching and prayers will end this side of heaven, but not worship, since God created us to worship Him. I have heard people complain about the type, style and tone of songs we sing in our churches. Many have been offended and some have even left the church because of their dissatisfaction with the song choices or styles selected by their worship teams. How sad. This is an age-old problem. There are still churches restricting the use of certain musical instruments for worship in services because they consider them unholy.

Once I was meditating on worship and asked God about it. This was because some older folks in the church I was attending felt the newer songs were too loud and upbeat. I can understand that this way of worshipping may have been unfamiliar. However, on the other hand, the younger people were tired of the old hymns and wanted something more modern. So, reflecting on this issue, I wondered what God thought about this topic. I was surprised by the mutterings I received within me during my personal contemplation. 'If God was not complaining, why were people so upset? .Worship is for Him and He looks into the hearts of worshippers to determine if their worship is acceptable or not. Worship is not for the singers or hearers; but for Him. Why the complaints when He holds no grievance on a subject so close to

His heart? In fact He can never have enough worship, because it pleases Him, and He intentionally seeks it!'

Worship could be compared to a little child who prepares breakfast in bed for a parent. The meal might not be great, and the taste might not be perfect, yet the parent is delighted because of the child's thoughtful consideration. The kitchen might be in disarray, and the child's clothing messy as a result of making the meal; still the parent would be ecstatic. So is God! We might not always present top-notch praise to God, yet He is delighted with our amateur efforts. Here is a Father seeking relationship with His children, therefore let us enjoy what the other brings to the house of God. We have no clue what worship songs we shall sing in heaven, however we know that in His presence there is fullness of joy!

Fun time in heaven

I am sure there will be time for humour in heaven, and I believe God will conduct a question and answer session. There might be people who are already well informed, but I think I would probably fall into the category of people with many questions. For example, I have a nagging question with regards to the marriage supper. I sometimes wonder if there would be lots of food served at the marriage feast in heaven between Christ and the Church. If the wedding is similar to the ones we have here, I assume we shall have lots to eat and drink like the wedding at Cana. What would we eat? Manna? Would we all be vegetarians since the lamb and the lion would play together? Does that mean there will be no steak at the wedding feast?

> 'The wolf also shall dwell with the lamb, and the leopard shall lie down with the kid; and the calf and the young lion and the fatling together; and

> a little child shall lead them. And the cow and the
> bear shall feed; their young ones shall lie down
> together: and the lion shall eat straw like the ox.
> And the sucking child shall play on the hole of the
> asp, and the weaned child shall put his hand on
> the cockatrice's den.'
>
> Isaiah 11:6-8

If we are feasting and celebrating together, who does the cooking? I wonder who would do the cleaning. I know nothing surprises God, and He makes all things beautiful in His time. The answers might be very obvious when we get to heaven. There will be lots of joy and laughter, so we shall need to be ready for this!

True worship

> 'But the hour cometh, and now is, when the true
> worshippers shall worship the Father in spirit and
> truth; for the Father seeketh such to worship
> him. God is a Spirit and they that worship Him
> must worship in spirit and in truth.'
>
> John 4:23-24

I still have much to learn on the subject of worship, because I am not disciplined enough to have prolonged personal worship sessions, except when driving in the car. I love to sing and worship but don't do it often enough. My son, Gboyega, is much better than me in praising God, because he takes his laptop with him everywhere, especially at weekends and in the mornings, listening to and participating in worship. I am always concerned about the effect of the steamy bathroom on electronics but that does not hinder my son.

I believe youths and young adults are very good at worshipping God, and we should invest in and nurture this ministry among young people because God longs for worship and fellowship. God looks to His creatures to bless Him with their voices.

The son of the morning, Lucifer, was an archangel responsible for worship in heaven, but he sinned and was thrown out of heaven:

> 'How art thou fallen from heaven, O Lucifer, son of the morning! How art thou cut down to ground, which didst weaken the nations! For thou hast said in thine heart, I will ascend into heaven, I will exalt my throne above the stars of God: I will sit also on the mount of the congregation, in the sides of the North: I will ascend above the heights of the clouds, I will be like the most High. Yet thou shalt be brought down to hell, to the sides of the Pit.'
>
> Isaiah 14:12-15

When Lucifer was expelled from heaven, God gave humans the privilege to praise and worship Him along with the angels and elders already in heaven. Unlike Angels, who were created as God's servants, we humans praise God out of our own free will. This means praise from us is usually born out of love, not out of duty. We are fortunate that God cannot resist praise from a sincere heart.

> 'But ye are a chosen generation, a royal priesthood, a holy nation, a peculiar people; that ye should shew forth the praises of Him who hath called you out of darkness into his marvelous light.'
>
> 1 Peter 2:9

I once heard an exposition explaining the praise and worship process using Solomon's temple, based on Psalm 100:4; 'Enter into His gates with thanksgiving, and into His courts with praise.' We approach God with thanksgiving and praise, as we progress in worship and adoration. This could be likened to gradually approaching the Holy place in Solomon's temple. Steady progress in this spiritual exercise of worshipping God leads us, as it were, towards the veil in the temple. As we pass through the veil which was torn in two when Jesus died on the cross, we enter the Holy place by the blood of the Lamb, focusing more on God and less on others. At this point, we personalise our encounter and approach the ark of the Covenant within the Holy of Holies. This new access was only made possible after Christ died and rose again, as indicated in the book of Hebrews:

> 'The Holy Ghost this signifying, that the way into the holiest of all was not yet made manifest, while as the first tabernacle was yet standing.'
>
> Hebrews 9:8

As we progress in worship, we sometimes attain a crescendo that culminates in silence before the throne of grace. 'Be still and know that I am God' - Psalm 46:10. Our spirits remain in awe of God as we reach the place of mystery, where humanity surrenders to divinity. At that moment, the Holy Spirit releases gifts and power,, we draw from this atmosphere in what we call, 'a time of ministry'. God speaks quietly to our souls, or loudly through prophesy to gatherings. We see visions, we witness miracles, we receive words of wisdom and words of knowledge. It becomes a time of personal and corporate blessing as in 1 Corinthians 12:7. At such times, it is good to stay calm and not grieve the Holy Spirit, but allow Him to take charge and operate at will. Unrestricted access with an atmosphere full of faith and exp ctation often culminates in transformed lives, needs being met, souls being saved and God glorified. Is that not the ultimate expression of the gospel?

> 'Whoso offereth praise glorifieth me; and to him that ordereth his conversation aright will I shew the salvation of God.'
>
> Psalm 50:23

Testimonies

In addition to participating in wonderful praise and worship, I have enjoyed listening to fantastic testimonies during my travels across Africa. Since there are hardly any time constraints in most African church services, sharing testimonies is a common feature welcomed by the congregation because it is the Bible coming alive! Testimonies create testimonies.

> 'And they overcame him by the blood of the Lamb, and by the word of their testimony; and they loved not their lives unto the death.'
>
> Revelation 12:11

Testimonies are important in demonstrating God's power in today's world. I understand that this might be open to abuse by unscrupulous people, however God is still God and there are many verifiable stories within His church. At a recent visit to a Methodist church in Uganda, a woman shared how God had provided a scholarship for her son to study law while she was having difficulty making ends meet. Another widow prayed to God and had a promotion at work so that she could take care of her two sons. Another woman thanked God for the special gift of a son, in addition to the two young daughters in her family. A bishop shared how God sent eleven Italian doctors to operate on his underweight son suffering from holes in his heart. His family could not raise the 1.5 million Kenyan Shillings needed for the operation, but God worked miraculously and the boy received the operation free of charge in Kenya. Twelve years on, the boy was still alive, and performing well at school. What a mighty God we serve!

Sharing testimonies is a thanksgiving gesture that glorifies God and makes Him relevant in today's world. It also helps the church grow, because it builds our faith to know that if God could do these things for someone else, He could also do them for us. Testimonies are also important for the less literate church members who find it difficult to study scriptures on their own.

Giving

I have heard all kinds of comments about tithing. Some say it is an Old Testament teaching, therefore it is obsolete and of no relevance in today's world. Another dear friend once told me she sends her tithe abroad, where it is needed most. I hear some split their tithes between various Christian agencies to support noble causes. I also understand that people withhold their tithes when unhappy with the church minister. Having not been taught about tithing, I was intrigued. At our university fellowship we discovered the truth about tithing in the Bible by ourselves, and it changed my life.

Having lived in the UK for some time now, I believe that there is insufficient teaching on 'money matters' in general. There is so much negativity about prosperity theology that the UK Church struggles to teach about finance and fundraising at all. It seems to be a taboo subject, perhaps for cultural reasons, and yet Christ spoke openly and frequently about money. This presents a serious problem for the future. If young people are not shown how to support the church, how will it sustain itself and continue its work?

Unfortunately the inability to openly discuss the subject of money has resulted in personal and family financial crises, and the modern 'credit culture' has resulted in debt issues for many members of our churches. This could have been prevented by better teaching on financial discipline and values. The church should be a safe place to discuss such issues so that parishioners do not fall prey to 'loan sharks' among other dangers. Thank God for organisations such as Christians Against Poverty (CAP), that offer free financial counselling and advice. How many young couples are being encouraged to take up financial classes as of marriage counselling? What does the Bible say about tithing and giving?

Feast of firstfruits

Recently at my church life group, we discussed the various feasts celebrated by Jews as commanded by the Lord in Leviticus 23. It was an interesting exercise as I could only recall a few of them from memory, and there are quite a number of feasts commanded by God.

They were collectively called the Feasts of the Lord; the Sabbath, Passover and the Feast of Unleavened Bread, the Feast of Firstfruits, the Feast of Weeks, the Feast of Trumpets, the Day of Atonement and the Feast of Tabernacles. Each feast has its own significance and I will leave you to explore this yourself in a study Bible if you are interested.

As I read through the Bible, I realised that many Old Testament practices reflect and reinforce modern day practices – for example, keeping the Sabbath day holy. Even though we now worship on the first day as opposed to the seventh day of the week, we still have a day of rest set apart to worship. Separating the first day of the week for worship helps commit the rest of the week to God and signifies giving the best part of the week to Him.

The feasts of Passover and Unleavened Bread support the celebration of Holy Communion, which is to be celebrated as often as possible in remembrance of the death of Christ. The third feast mentioned in Leviticus 23 is the Feast of Firstfruits. When I consider how the Jews celebrate their feasts, there is still so much I still need to learn about God and His priorities. He is a God of work, but He also prioritises rest, and He honours those who obey Him because God's foolishness outweighs the wisdom of man.

> 'Speak unto the children of Israel, and say unto them, when ye be come into the land which I give unto you, and shall reap the harvest thereof, then ye shall bring a sheaf of the firstfruits of your harvest unto the priest. And he shall wave the sheaf before the Lord, to be accepted for you: on the morrow after the sabbath the priest shall wave it. And ye shall offer that day when ye wave the sheaf and a 'he lamb' (male) without blemish of the first year for a burnt offering unto the Lord. And the meant offering thereof shall be two tenth deals of fine flour mingled with oil, an offering made by fire unto the Lord for a sweet savour: and the drink offering thereof shall be of wine, the fourth part of an hin (a gallon of wine). And ye shall eat neither bread nor parched corn, nor green ears, until the selfsame day that ye have brought an offering unto your God: it shall be a statute forever throughout your generations in all your dwellings.'
>
> Leviticus 23:10-14 (explanation in bracket)

This passage demonstrates to me that God wishes to be honoured by giving Him first place in our lives and particularly in our possessions, so that we do not make gods out of our riches. I believe a similar principle operates in the New Testament.

Tithes

What is tithe and how is it related to the Feast of Firstfruits in the Old Testament?

> 'Thus speak unto the Levites, and say to them, When ye take of the children of Israel the tithes which I have given you from them for your inheritance, then ye shall offer up a heave offering of it for the Lord, even a tenth part of the tithe.'
>
> Numbers 18:26

The tithe, which is a tenth of our earnings, is to be brought to the house of God so there is provision in His house. The Levites, who could be likened to ministers, pastors or vicars, were supported by the tithes brought to the temple, synagogue or church. Out of the resources made available to the Levites, Moses instructed the Levites to also offer a heave (peace) offering to the Lord. So the tithe principle is applicable to both laity and the ordained.

I learnt the significance of paying tithe at my campus fellowship. To start with, we student members of the campus fellowship had to support ourselves because there was no funding from any church or external organisation. We read the Bible and discovered that God expected us to support His work and further the gospel. We also needed to share Holy Communion regularly as indicated in Acts 2:46. So funds were raised from personal allowances for this important commandment. As students, we also visited other campuses on evangelistic outreaches, offered support to the poor and needy, including students on campus and outside. We decided to bring ten percent of our monthly allowances as a minimum, in addition to the offerings given during fellowship and outreaches. Over thirty years on, I am always grateful for the blessings and discipline that this command has brought to my life.

> 'Will a man rob God? Yet ye have robbed me. But ye say, 'Wherein have we robbed thee?' In tithes and offerings. Ye are cursed with a curse: for ye have robbed me, even this whole nation. Bring ye **ALL** the tithes into the storehouse, that there may be meat in mine house, prove me now herewith, saith the Lord of Hosts if I will not open you the windows of heaven, and pour you out a blessing, that there shall not be room enough to receive it. And I will rebuke the devourer for your sakes, and he shall not destroy the fruits of your ground; neither shall your vine cast her fruit before the time in the field, saith the Lord of hosts. And all nations shall call you blessed: for ye shall be a delightsome land, saith the Lord of hosts.'
>
> Malachi 3:8-12

Ministers do their members a disservice if they do not teach them to honour God with their lives and possessions. Tithe, which is ten percent of our income, is the least we can give God, if we profess that He owns all we have. The question therefore is, are we reliable? Can God rely on us to extend His kingdom on earth both spiritually and practically? The tax man deducts his percentage of our income in the UK to fund national services.

God, on the other hand, asks us to bring the tithe cheerfully and willingly, so that He can bless and protect us. He does not force us against our will. So, when do we bring our tithes?

> 'Honour the Lord with substance, and with the firstfruits of all thine increase. So shall thy barns be filled with plenty, and thy presses shall burst out with new wine.'
>
> Proverbs 3:9

Today, many Christians set up standing orders to ensure regular and timely payments into their church bank accounts. This is helpful, as it prevents us from giving the dregs of our income, and ensures that we present our firstfruits, honouring God. For those who still wish to manually bring the tithe to the storehouse, it might be beneficial to withdraw and see the money aside before making other payments to avoid degrading the tithe. It is also a good idea to speak to the tithe, thank God for His provision and take the opportunity to rebuke the devourer (plunderer) so you become fruitful in every part of your life.

Honouring God with your tithe also fulfils Jesus' command in the New Testament. 'But seek ye first the kingdom of God, and His righteousness; and all these things shall be added unto you.' Matthew 6:33. As we seek and serve God with our lives and our wealth, we benefit from our covenant through Jesus. How?

The less is blessed of the better. In Hebrews Chapter 7, Abraham was blessed by Melchisedec, King of Salem (Peace) and a High Priest. Abraham voluntarily and happily gave a tenth of all his wealth to Melchisedec without any law or compulsion and he was blessed. It only makes sense to voluntarily and happily offer all this to Jesus our Prince of Peace and High Priest after the order of Melchisedec. Consequently we reap what we sow. When we sow spiritually, we reap spiritual blessings just as when we sow physically, we also reap physical blessings. Where our hearts are, there our treasures will be. We should not give grudgingly or of necessity, because God loves a cheerful giver.

What about splitting our tithes? Can we send our tithe abroad? In Malachi 3:8-12 it appears that the tithe is for the storehouse alone. The passage instructs us to bring **all** the tithe, not some! Where is the storehouse? God called the storehouse His house – the church or gathering of the people, not the building. The storehouse is where we are being fed and ministered to spiritually.

If you receive more than one income, or receive various gifts, then it is your decision how you handle that. I believe God's aim is to make us responsible for the upkeep and resourcing of our spiritual home and His servants or else we are robbing God.

The good news is that when we honour our Father with our tithes and offerings, we invite His blessings on our finances and lifestyle. Over the years the significant outpouring for me has been His wisdom and favour in life matters. I won a scholarship that was worth thousands of pounds to study at Edinburgh University when I was a civil servant. I could not have saved up the money myself. Recently I purchased an almost new vehicle at an amazing price and was given an interest-free car loan by a relative. A few months earlier, I bought a house I thought I could not afford in a beautiful neighbourhood at an astonishing price. It was a miraculous because I obtained a unique mortgage deal that ended almost immediately!

It does not end there. God rebukes the devourer for our sake. I remember going away from home for four days. On my return, I saw my house keys still hanging from the keyhole of my front door, and no one had been inside the house! It was by His grace that I was not burgled. I remember at the start of the 2008 recession, the Spirit instructed me to cash in my 'Individual Savings Account' shares investment just before the market downturn – it was a life saver for me. I did not lose my savings, and was able to use them wisely. I have enjoyed so much protection from the spiritual devourer and God has helped me enjoy several harvests in this life.

Lastly, the scriptures state that all nations shall call us blessed, which means God's favour will be evident in our lives. God's favour often has nothing to do with our intelligence or ability, rather it is God guiding us to be in the right place at the right time. What others scramble for, could easily become ours. That is favour, and not only for us, but for members of our family too.

Offerings

Offerings are our gifts over and above our tithe. Paying tithes and offerings have never been mandatory, always optional. However, He told the Israelites in 1 Samuel:

> 'Wherefore the Lord God of Israel saith, I said indeed that thy house, and the house of thy father, should walk before me forever: but now the Lord saith: Be it far from me; for them that honour me I will honour, and they that despise me shall be lightly esteemed.'
>
> 1 Samuel 2:30

God ensures that He honours those who honour Him. It is not the amount that counts, but obedience to His command. He prefers we give ourselves before giving our tithe, since we do not honour Him if we only give our tithes and offerings yet have no time to worship Him, or fellowship with others in the house of the Lord.

Questions to ponder

- ❖ Do I take time out to worship God in spirit and truth?
- ❖ How often do I testify about His goodness in my life?
- ❖ How faithful am I in paying my tithes and offerings?

Amen, amen
Blessings and glory
Wisdom thanksgiving
And honour
Power and might
Be unto the Lord
Forever and ever
Amen

Corpers fellowship ~ Nigeria

CHAPTER 5

Prayer of Faith

'And this is the confidence that we have in Him
that, if we ask any thing according to His will,
he heareth us: And if we know that He hear us,
whatsoever we ask, we know that we have the
petitions that we desired of Him.'

1 John 5:14-15

The central issue for me as a believer in my undergraduate
years was establishing and growing my faith. I read books,
recited scriptures and sang songs about faith. Without faith, it
is impossible to please God, so I fed my faith by studying and
listening to inspiring teachings. In Nigeria in the early eighties,
I was influenced by great servants of God who visited Ibadan
University campus regularly. Pastor Enoch Adeboye, Senior
Pastor of the Redeemed Christian Church of Christ, came at
least one night a month to teach us in a large auditorium.

Archbishop Benson Idahosa led crusades in Ibadan at various
large venues. I attended one of these, and that was the first time
in my life I personally saw miracles. People walked from their
wheelchairs, the blind saw, the lame walked, delivered brothers

and sisters were praising God. It was incredible. I stood in awe, and the book of the Acts of the Apostles became real to me. I was ready to live a life of faith! It was not a film or hearsay, I had witnessed God in action, and that brought my faith to a higher dimension.

Challenge of Faith

School was good, I was doing well in my undergraduate course and I was growing spiritually. I attended fellowship regularly and shared my faith with enthusiasm. Things were going well. Then at the end of the semester, I went home. I arrived in the evening but mum was not expecting me, so no one was at home. Our house was a large, beautiful semi-detached property near the motorway leading to the international airport in Lagos. My parents were separated and my other siblings were at their universities and grammar school. There was no mobile phone to communicate with anyone. I retrieved the spare key from neighbours living behind our house and went upstairs to drop my bags in my bedroom

As I came out, I noticed a small black talisman just above the first floor exit door onto the balcony. I wondered what it was, and how it got there. I thought to myself, 'The light of God shines, and no darkness can overcome it'. I removed the charm, went outside and threw it into dense vegetation growing on undeveloped land not far from the house.

Shortly afterwards, my mum returned home and was delighted to see me. She went upstairs, noticed that the charm was missing, and was livid! She told me that since she was not the only one at home, she had to pay a large sum of money for protection against armed robberies due to the location of our house. I told mum, that Jesus would protect her. At that time she was a Muslim. She said that she had no problem with Him protecting her, but heaven also helps those who help themselves. She was in no mood for any preaching at all. She insisted on getting back her talisman or sending me to my dad's house. I had thrown the charm away, buzzing with my new-found faith, ready to prove the Lordship of Christ! I told her that I loved and respected her and would pray for her protection, but that the talisman was gone. She did not believe me, and thought I was stubbornly refusing to hand it back.

So I left home at about eight o'clock that evening. My dad lived at Ojota, Lagos, about an hour from my mum's house, so I decided to go back to Ibadan University instead. I had never slept at dad's house, and was not prepared to choose him and my stepmother over my mum. Even though her belief system was different from mine, she was still my mum and had always supported us! So with five naira left in my pocket, I took the last public bus back to Ibadan. I told myself that 'when my father and mother forsake me, then the Lord will take me up'. (Psalm 27:10).

I arrived in Ibadan at midnight and hitchhiked to the university. Looking back now, my bold determination was reckless! I reached campus and went to my room, I had no money, and decided that I would have to live by faith. Each morning I prayed to the Father to provide for me. Whenever I managed to get fifty kobo from friends, equivalent to fifty pence, I bought a few mangoes, and ate one for breakfast, one for lunch and one for dinner. At weekends, quite a lot of wedding receptions took place in the hall within my hall of residence, so I was able to eat free food because everyone is invited to weddings. I survived until my Christian friends returned to school after a few weeks but still could not bring myself to ask for financial assistance, because I was from a fairly well-to-do family, and did not want to lie about the reason for leaving home. As a result I was losing weight, and my friends thought I was on some kind of diet. Eventually a few of my Christian friends approached me, saying that the Holy

Spirit had urged them to bless me financially. I was so grateful that He did care for me.

Throughout this time, I did not know where my next meal was coming from, but our heavenly Father was faithful. I learnt how to be observant, how to identify the signs of those in need and to live by faith. It also taught me the importance of being generous to those facing hardship or in less fortunate positions than myself.

A few months after I left home, my mum saw my dad. She was raging because she thought I had been staying in his house, and that he had not reprimanded me. My dad said that he had not seen me, and he came to visit me at university. I was at fellowship that Sunday, so he left money and food for me! I was thrilled, and shared my testimony at the fellowship the following week. I not only experienced His providence, I also realised the importance of funding God's storehouse to help the poor live a in dignified way. I thank Him for his safeguarding principles to this day.

Divine intervention

My life is an encyclopedia of miracles, my Heavenly Father has been so good and kind to me. I remember, before I became pregnant with my second child, asking God for a daughter because I already had a son. I had access to a scan but decided not to know the gender of the baby until birth. When the expected delivery date arrived, there was no sign of labour. I waited all day but the baby was in no hurry to come out. Later that night, I noticed that the very big and active baby had become inactive. I cried out to God and told him that I didn't want a still birth, asking Him to show me that the baby was still alive. With my hand on my stomach, I could feel her move a little, though it was very slight. I was very anxious and hardly slept, expecting labour to begin at any time, and tossing and turning in an effort to find a comfortable position. Very early the next morning, I told my husband, Ade to take me to the general hospital at Minna- Nigeria. At about five o'clock in the morning the midwife checked the baby and told me that she was in breech position; lying transversely instead of vertically with the head engaged. She suggested I waited for the consultant who was expected on site at seven o'clock. Dr Fash, the consultant, carried out a scan and was very concerned. If there was no change of the situation by ten o'clock, he would have to perform a Caesarean operation. He said the baby showed signs of severe distress. He could not rule out the possibility of disability, and the baby had to be born soon. Even though I wanted the baby out as soon as possible, I also had a sixteen-month-old son at home, so I did not want to go through an emergency Caesarean.

After meeting with the consultant, I was taken to the maternity ward at the general hospital at around nine o'clock in the morning. It was a communal ward with several other pregnant mothers. I stood up and started walking up and down the ward, but Ade had to stay outside. I started confessing out loud, reminding God that the Hebrew mothers were able to deliver their babies before the Egyptian midwives arrived, and their babies were healthy and strong. 'God, I believe you can do it again. Please cause this child to descend in the right orientation so she can be born normally, with no complications. Thank you for my miracle baby. I shall testify of your greatness.'

At around half past nine, the midwife came to check on my progress. If I was not in labour, I would be taken to the theatre whilst Ade was sent to the pharmacy to purchase medication to induce labour. The midwife was surprised to find that I was already in the second stage of labour, though without any contraction pains. I was taken to the delivery room and by half past ten my daughter had come shrieking into the world, weighing about ten pounds. I thanked the Lord. That was my last delivery, and my daughter was completely perfect. Ironically, today she is a junior doctor working in an obstetrics and gynaecology department in England, delivering babies. Glory be to God! 'Death and life are in the power of the tongue: and they that love it shall eat the fruit thereof.' Proverbs 18:21. If you can conceive it, you can achieve it.

Miraculous move

I will share one more miracle to prove that, with faith, all things are possible. The Bible says: 'The fear of the wicked, it shall come upon him: but the desire of the righteous shall be granted,'Proverbs 10:24

I was commuting from Witney in Oxfordshire, to my work in London. I parked my car at the Thornhill Park & Ride, where I took the London coach every morning. I spent about two and a half hours travelling each way. Initially, car parking was free, but a few years later we were being charged by the day. The long commuting time to work, plus the new car parking charges made me decide to sell my flat. I found an immediate buyer, but the paperwork and legal wrangling by my estate agents delayed its sale by nine months. The housing market was overheating but the week before exchanging contracts, in November 2013, my vendors took their house off the market. The following week the property was back on market with a price increase of £20,000. My solicitor advised that I either defer the sale of my property or increase its sale price to reflect the current housing market. I felt it was unfair to change the sale price after agreement with my buyer earlier in the year, despite the increase in market value. So I stuck to my decision to sell at the original price, and move on. However, my job required frequent journeys out of the UK making it increasingly difficult to agree a final date to exchange contracts. By the middle of November 2013, the documents to be updated by the management company were still pending so I prayed for a breakthrough, and took a step of faith!

I needed to sell the flat to help support my daughter in her final year of medical school and help pay my son's postgraduate maintenance costs at Lund University in Sweden. I needed money by December 2013 at the latest to avoid having to obtain a loan for these expenses. By the end of November, I had a strong urge to start packing. I booked a van for the following week and told my solicitor I was moving out on the sixth of December. I left the keys to the flat with the estate agent, even though my solicitor advised against it. Leaving the keys without exchanging contracts was a high risk move, but I was willing to move forward by faith! I placed my possessions in storage, moved into a friend's flat in Oxford, gave my solicitor the power of attorney to sell the property and travelled out of the UK. By the time I returned in late December, the long-awaited documents were still pending, but the exchange had taken place.

Some money was withheld as collateral, but I was able to pay the college expenses for both children without getting a loan. The extra would be the deposit for the new house, nevertheless where would it be, and how much would it cost? House prices were skyrocketing and I was house hunting every week, when I could. At that time, a two bedroomed property near London attracted 60 viewings in one day. I made four offers for four different properties, but they all fell through.

Estate agents across the country were having a field day. My mortgage adviser was an angel, and very patient and kind to me. I had to send texts and emails as soon as instructed by him, due to fierce competition for the available properties, but I never gave up. I was conscious that I gave my friend no deadline to leave, however I did not want to overstay my welcome at her small flat. I prayed to God, asking for favour and direction at this trying time, because I knew no estate agent would assist me. Then I travelled to Europe for a conference over the weekend.

On my way back at the end of January 2014, I called an estate agent about a property I had seen online while in Sweden. I prayed for a miracle to secure it, even though I had not seen the house. It was located close to the M40 and not far from Watford, where my sister used to live. The estate agent said there were 13 interested viewers, though I arrived first. To cut a long story short, I the property price was £30,000 above my initial budget; nonetheless, it was a beautiful bungalow. By mid-March 2014, I had moved in! It was the Lord's doing again. He made it all beautiful (though nerve wracking) in His time (Ecclesiastes 3:11).

Prayers of faith have no alternative, only absolute trust that He will do what He says He will do. Without faith, it is impossible to please God, therefore either He intervenes or you are finished. Prayers of faith require an expectation that He will keep His promises through the rough times of faith journeys. Faith is not moved by what we see or feel, for these are temporal. Faith is eternal, because it is based on God's word and His character. Have faith in God.

> 'And Jesus answering saith unto them, Have faith in God. Therefore I say unto you, 'What things so ever ye desire, when ye pray, believe that ye rece ive them, and ye shall have them.'
>
> Mark 11: 22, 24

Questions to ponder

- ❖ How do I challenge my faith?
- ❖ What do I need to stretch my faith?
- ❖ How often do I look out for others in need of assistance?

Choma, Zambia

Prayer for Healing

'How God anointed Jesus of Nazareth with the Holy Ghost and with power: who went about doing good, and healing all that were oppressed of the devil; for God was with him. And we are witnesses of all things which he did both in the land of the Jews, and in Jerusalem; whom they slew and hanged on a tree.'

Acts 2:38-39

I remember when, I newly arrived in the UK years ago, I could not understand why many churches were sceptical of divine healing. It was as if God could only perform miracles through medical professionals, and the era of divine healing by prayers and laying on of hands was long gone. On the other hand, there were healing services being conducted by evangelical, charismatic and Pentecostal churches in the UK.

Having recently arrived from Africa, the hallmarks of Christianity for me were salvation through Christ supported by miracles, and the most common miracles I had previously encountered were miracles of healing. In the great commission in Mark 16, it states clearly that these signs shall follow believers:

> 'And He said unto them, 'Go ye into all the world, and preach the gospel to every creature. He that believeth and is baptized shall be saved; but he that believeth not shall be damned. And these signs shall follow them that believe. In my name they shall cast out devils; they shall speak with new tongues, they shall take up serpents; and if they drink any deadly thing, it shall not hurt them; **they shall lay hands on the sick, and they shall recover.**'
>
> Mark 16:15-18, emphasis added

Signs following believers

1. One of the signs following believers is the laying on of hands when praying for the sick, and seeing the sick recover. In my experience and understanding, there are various types of afflictions – physical, emotional, psychological, mental and spiritual afflictions that may be caused by stress, diseases or demonic activity as mentioned in Mark 16 above. Healing occurs where there is faith in Jesus for healing. This might be at healing services, or prayers at hospitals, at evangelistic outreaches, at homes or where faith is demonstrated. For example, Christ prayed for Peter's mother-in-law and she was healed of fever and she got up and served them.

   'But Simon's wife's mother lay sick of a fever, and anon thy tell him of her. And he came and took her by the hand, and lifted her up; and immediately the fever left her, and she ministered unto them.'

Mark 1:30-31

2. Healing was described by Jesus as children's bread.

    'Then came she and worshipped Him, saying, 'Lord, help me'. But he answered and said, 'It is not meet to take the children's bread, and to cast it to dogs'. And she said, 'Truth, Lord: yet the dogs eat of the crumbs which fall from their masters' table'. Then Jesus answered and said unto her, 'O woman, great is thy faith: be it unto thee even as thou wilt'. And her daughter was made whole from that very hour.'

    Matthew 15:25-30

The daughter was healed because her mother had faith despite being a gentile. A gentile benefited from Jewish entitlements during Christ's ministry, even though He came primarily to the Jews, with the hope of blessing the whole world eventually. Jesus could not resist responding to faith, thereby blessing this Canaanite woman before her time. Therefore healing could take place anywhere faith in Christ exists or where His power is present to heal. In this case there was no laying on of hands or physical touch.

3. On another occasion, Jesus responded to the faith of four men seeking healing their friend as they lowered him through the roof to present him to Christ when He was teaching in a Pharisee's house. It was the faith of the friends that captured His attention: "And it came to pass on a certain day, as he was teaching, that there were Pharisees and doctors of the law sitting by, which

were come out of every town of Galilee, and Judaea, and Jerusalem: and **the power of the Lord was present to heal them.** And, behold, men brought in a bed a man which was taken with a palsy: and they sought means to bring him in, and to lay him before Him. And when they could not find by what way they might bring him in because of the multitude, they went upon the housetop, and let him down through the tiling with his couch into the midst before Jesus. And **when He saw their faith**, He said unto him, 'Man, thy sins are forgiven thee.'

Luke 5:17-20

4. Personal faith - there was no third party request in the account of the woman with the issue of blood. She was in a desperate condition, having spent much time and money seeking a solution for her condition. It was not only a medically challenging situation, her condition also hampered her social life, because her social, because she was considered unclean in Jewish culture. Her deep concern gave her special faith in Jesus for immediate healing. In fact, she had no intention of asking Him directly for healing. She was content to be healed anonymously until Jesus sensed faith drawing virtue from Him: 'And behold, a woman, which was diseased with an issue of blood twelve years, came behind him, and touched the hem of His garment.' Matthew 9:20

We know there were many others around Jesus on this occasion, yet nothing happened to them because they had no expectation of healing, but she did!

5. In an entirely different setting, it was the attitude and words of the centurion that Jesus admired in Matthew 8:10. 'When Jesus heard it, He marveled, and said to

them that followed, "Verily, I say unto you, I have not found so great faith, no, not in Israel." Healing is a demonstration of His love for humanity irrespective of race, gender, creed, tribe or tongue.

6. Under another circumstance, as by the pool of Bethesda, a lame man had been waiting for healing for over thirty years. He was healed because of mercy. There was no mention of his faith although Christ must have perceived his hopelessness and responded with compassion.

   'And a certain man was there, which had an infirmity thirty and eight years. When Jesus saw him lie, and knew that he had been now a long time in that case, he saith unto him, 'Wilt thou be made whole?' The impotent man answered him, 'Sir, I have no man, when the water is troubled, to put me into the pool: but while I am coming, another steppeth down before me'. Jesus saith unto him, 'Rise, take up thy bed, and walk'. And immediately the man was made whole, and took up his bed, and walked: and on the same day was the Sabbath.'

   John 5:5-7

This narrative is an example of people without faith experiencing miraculous healing due to divine mercy.

Healing virtue

Acts of divine healing are never predictable because only God sees the heart, and He seeks permission from no one before unleashing love and compassion. All through my Christian journey,

I have seen sick people healed by proclaiming the word of God, and others experienced no healing despite having faith in Him. This is a mystery. Believers and unbelievers have been healed at crusades and evangelistic outreaches, with or without the laying on of hands. Psalm 107:20 declares that God 'sent his word, and healed them, and delivered them from their destructions whilst the Israelites were still in the wilderness. Power still prevails in His word, as long as there is faith in His name.

In the New Testament, healing virtue was reported to flow when Jesus taught the crowd or shared the Holy scriptures. In recent times, healing virtue flows during corporate worship, when sharing testimonies and after great and inspiring teaching! The Messiah often spent time expounding scriptures to reveal His love for humanity before performing miracles. Faith comes by hearing God's word again and again. It is therefore the atmosphere of faith that generates expectations and strengthens convictions. When prayers are made in faith, healing virtue begins to flow by His Spirit and anointing released for ministry.

Administering healing through prayers

1. There was an exchange at Calvary. What does that mean? Jesus paid the debt for 'sin' and 'sickness' so we may obtain right standing with God called 'righteousness' and 'healing'. It could be likened to a twin agreeing to swap places with his brother that had a death sentence in order to free him to live and provide for his young family. The swap was only possible when the guilty accepts the offer to escape punishment and the authority allows it. God allowed and authorised the swap on the cross

of Calvary between Jesus and every sinner. Whenever we confess that we deserve the punishment for sin but appropriate the death of Jesus to take our place, exchange takes place at Calvary.

'For the wages of sin is death; but the gift of God is eternal life through Jesus Christ our Lord'.

Romans 6:23

2. Nevertheless there are occasions when God heals through prayers even though recipients are not Christians. Irrespective of the situation, the stripes Jesus bore on our behalf before his crucifixion makes healing available to humanity. 1 Peter 2:24 'Who his own self bare our sins in his own body on the tree, that we, being dead to sins, should live unto righteousness: by whose stripes ye were healed'.

3. Healing can be gradual or instant, d pending on the anointing available at the moment of prayer and ministry. As we tune to His Spirit, He guides us into truth and reveals His purpose and ways. In Psalm 103:7 God made His ways known to Moses, but His acts to the children of Israel. As we mature in Christ, God reveals His acts, His ways, and His purposes as we serve as His servants.

4. When praying for others, where possible it is sometimes good to enquire what is needed, because things are not always as they appear. In Mark 10 we encounter blind Bartimaeus:

'And Jesus answered and said unto him, 'What wilt thou that I should do unto thee?'. The blind man said unto him, 'Lord, that I might receive my

sight'. And Jesus said unto him, 'Go thy way; thy
faith hath made thee whole'. And immediately he
received his sight, and followed Jesus in the way.'

Mark 10:51-52

One could say it was obvious that Bartimaeus was blind, but
being physically healed might not have been his priority, hence
Jesus asked him.

5. The cause of the problem might sometimes be hidden.
    For example, an insomniac unable to sleep, might be
    suffering from stress. As we pray for healing, we might
    need to listen on various levels to know the cause of the
    affliction, both from the person who has sought prayer
    and the Holy Spirit. If the insomnia was due to anxiety
    for instance, the person might be encouraged to read
    and confess affirming scriptures such as Proverbs 3.
    Hopefully the scriptures would help address issues of
    anxiety or fear.

    'When thou liest down, thou shalt not be afraid;
    yea, thou shalt lie down, and thy sleep shall be
    sweet. Be not afraid of sudden fear, neither of
    the desolation of the wicked when it cometh. For
    the Lord will be thy confidence...

    'Proverbs 3:24-26.

6. If the sleeplessness requires lifestyle adjustment as
    stated below.:'It is vain for you to rise up early, to sit
    up late, to eat the bread of sorrows; **for so he gives his
    beloved sleep.**' Psalm 127:2. Then the subject might
    have to think seriously about time management.

7. If God was trying to get the person's attention, as was the case with Samuel, I do not believe it would be a prolonged process. Eventually He will get the person's attention and life should revert to normal. We need to stay humble, open and obedient during healing ministry.

8. If you are praying for someone and cannot discern anything, then just pray as directed by scriptures and let God to do the rest. Join your faith with the person's, share a simple prayer and move on. I love this principle described by the apostle Paul when ministering to people:

   "For our rejoicing is this, the testimony of our conscience, that in simplicity and godly sincerity, not with fleshly wisdom, but by the grace of God, we have had our conversation in the world, and more abundantly to you ward.'
   2 Corinthians 1:12

I should reiterate that no one can predict how the Holy Spirit will operate. We pray to the Father in Jesus' name, based on His words through the power of His Spirit. It is not the length of prayer that matters, but the faith behind it.

We should signpost requests to Jesus whilst being kind and sensitive. Sometimes the human relations side of things might take time, for example to establish trust, understand the issue and determine how to pray. However, the prayer itself can be short and straight to the point. I find Jesus' prayers very brief – 'rise up and walk', 'be healed', 'take up thy bed', 'you are forgiven'. The Pharisees shared long convoluted prayers to seek attention and recognition, but Jesus spoke simply and with conviction.

Our prayers should be spoken with authority, backed by expectation, motivated by compassion and then left to the healer for the outcome. In Acts 9:33-34, Peter met Aeneas who was bed-ridden and paralysed. All he said was 'Jesus Christ maketh thee whole; arise and make thy bed.' Aeneas was healed instantly. Short and confident prayers honour Christ and elicit faith in the hearer.

Ministry gifts as adjuncts

Other ministry gifts operate with prayers for healing. For instance, during counselling or enquiry sessions, we might need to **discern** hidden causes, for example bitterness, immaturity or issues requiring forgiveness. At other times, asking the right questions can expose the root problem, such as exposure to unhelpful materials including pornography or occult practices. Perhaps the problem requires cancelling generational ties or breaking covenant ties to organisations such as the freemasons. A word of knowledge, a word of wisdom or the discernment of Spirits gives essential insight to those ministering in prayer. Again, the subject should be referred to key scriptures and encouraged to immerse themselves in God's word, to build up faith and equip themselves to take every thought captive in future.

On other occasions, the person called to pray could operate in the special gift of faith or gift of miracles. A simple prayer of faith for the sick or the dead, if stirred by the Holy Spirit, can bring a person back to life. Peter was called to pray for Tabitha in Acts 9:40-41 when she was sick and later died. The widows sent for him, and he met them crying in the room. Peter asked them all to leave the room, knelt down and prayed. All he said was 'Tabitha, arise' and she did. Does this not sound like the time when Jesus prayed for the only daughter or a Jewish leader in Matthew 9:23-26? It is the authority we have in Christ that gives the confidence and supports our expectations. Some refer to this as special faith'.

When I read about healings, I believe this was what Jesus meant in John 14:12, 'Verily, verily, I say unto you, He that believeth in me, the works that I do shall he do also; and greater works than these shall he do; because I go unto my Father'. I wonder if He expects us to perform more miracles than He did, because he had only three years of ministry. That is a tall order, as the Church still struggles with operating in these basic ministry gifts.

Other ministry gifts associated with the gift of healing are words of wisdom and words of knowledge. At some outreach events, I have observed the evangelist or minister experiencing pain in the knee or back and announcing it to the congregation. 'There is someone here with a sharp pain the right knee', and people come out of their places for prayer. Words of knowledge often relates to things to come, whereas words of wisdom are often about the present or past. For example, there might be a word of knowledge about someone with a difficult pregnancy, where prayer is needed to avert complications, or to alert people about an impending event.

In the passage below, the Lord appears to Ananias and instructs him to go and pray for Saul that he may receive his sight. The Lord also appears to Saul, explaining that Ananias would come from Damascus to pray for his healing by the laying on of hands. Even though Saul was a new Christian, both men manifested ministry gifts that resulted in healing.

> 'And there was a certain disciple at Damascus named Ananias; and to him said the Lord in a vision, Ananias. And he said, 'Behold, I am here, Lord.' And the Lord said unto him, 'Arise, and go into the street which is called Straight, and enquire in the house of Judas for one called Saul,

of Tarsus': for, behold, he prayeth. And hath seen
in a vision a man named Ananias coming in, and
putting his hand on him, that he might receive
his sight.'

Acts 9: 10-12

Holy Communion and healing

Another means of receiving healing is to participate in Holy
Communion. In Isaiah 53:5 we are told that by the stripes of
Jesus' (the wounds and punishment He received on our behalf
at the cross) we are healed. We are given healing in exchange
for sickness because He took our sorrows and pain at Calvary.
He was broken for us, therefore as we break bread, eat it and
drink the wine, we celebrate His victory over sin, sickness, pain
and death!

Holy Communion is a powerful sacrament that restores life,
and brings healing in many ways when we believe. As we partake
in this sacred event, we should claim our healing and health in
Jesus' name. He said 'do this in remembrance of me'; what a
Saviour!

Anointing oil and healing

The use of the anointing oil dates back to the time of Moses
in Exodus 37:29, when the people of Israel were building the tent
of tabernacle in the wilderness. On occasions where there is no
anointing oil, Holy Communion has been proven to facilitate
healing as described above. However, the Bible encouraged early
church leaders to anoint the sick with oil and pray for healing.

'Is anyone among you afflicted? Let him pray. Is any merry? Let him sing psalms. Is any sick among you? Let him call for the elders of the church; and let them pray over him, anointing him with oil in the name of the Lord. And the prayer of faith shall save the sick, and the Lord shall raise him up; and if he have committed sins, they shall be forgiven him.'

James 5:13-15

We should encourage one another to ask for prayer when going through suffering or difficult times. In addition, we can ask the church elders to anoint us with oil and pray for Healing. The power of agreement among believers plus corporate authority vested in the elders: draws healing through the anointing oil and the laying on if hands.

As a word of caution, it is important to know the church leader or person praying for you, or to be sure of his or her reputation to ensure that only genuine disciples of Christ draw upon the healing power of our Lord. Seek prayer in trustworthy surroundings as instructed in 1 Timothy 5:22, 'Lay hands suddenly on no man, neither be partakers of other men's sins; keep yourself pure.'

Confessional prayers

In James 5:16, we are encourage to 'Confess your faults to one another, and pray for one another, that ye may be healed. fte effective, fervent prayer of a righteous man availeth much'. James advises us to confess our sins to one another, and then pray for one another. Confessing to close Christian friends helps promote close, accountable relationships, and ensures we do not take grace for granted. Bear in mind that, sometimes, healing may be hampered until confession is made. Unforgiveness, resentment, malice, envy, and other hard-hearted positions must be acknowledged before they can be effectively addressed, thus initiating healing and restoration.

> 'If we say that we have no sin, we deceive ourselves, and the truth is not in us. If we confess our sins, He is faithful and just to forgive us our sins, and to cleanse us from all unrighteousness. If we say that we have not sinned, we make Him a liar, and His word is not in us.'
>
> 1 John 1:8-10

The goal of the confession referred to here is divine cleansing, which helps us lead a stronger Christian walk. This confession is made directly to God, and He forgives us our sins no matter how bad. However, forgiveness does not mean we avoid the consequences of our actions; for example, if you start a fight, your opponent may forgive you when you repent. Nonetheless you might still have to pay the penalty for assault. In a similar way, a person might confess an anger problem to a close Christian friend, for accountability; but an anger management class with prayer plus accountability may be needed manage the situation effectively. The ultimate goal of confessional prayers is to make us better Christians, with clear consciences and with nothing held back to mar our relationship with God.

Praise and worship

Two key ingredients of the healing meetings I have attended are expectation and worship. If people come expecting to be healed, then expectation works closely with faith. Expectation is particularly high among those unable to afford healthcare, making God their first or only resort. Praise and worship attract divine presence as well as angelic performance. As we worship Him, a healing anointing is released and people may experience healing spontaneously, even without being touched or prayed for. I have seen physically disabled people walk out of their wheelchairs during worship and others get delivered without anyone ministering to them. At some outreach events, the leader may invite people to share their testimonies of healings experienced during worship and prayers. At other times, the wind of healing blows across the venue and healing is experienced irrespective of background or even belief.

Healing the land

Healing the land and the effect of this on the people is an interesting topic explored in 2 Chronicles 30:18-20.

> 'For a multitude of the people, even many from Ephraim, and Manasseh, Issachar, and Zebulun, had not cleansed themselves, yet did they eat the Passover otherwise than it was written. But Hezekiah prayed for them, saying, 'The good Lord pardon every one that prepareth his heart to seek God, the Lord God of his fathers, though he be not cleansed according to the purification of the sanctuary'. And the Lord hearkened to Hezekiah, and healed the people.'

The Israelites had forsaken God for so long and worshipped other gods, therefore they were oppressed by their enemies and taken captive. However, Hezekiah decided to celebrate the Passover in the same way as in the time of Solomon. He invited all the tribes of Israel and Judah and asked the Levites and priests to consecrate themselves. More than a thousand bulls were slaughtered in addition to lambs. The people called upon Jehovah but not all had consecrated themselves. Hezekiah interceded on their behalf and He hearkened **and healed the people.** There was celebration for fourteen days as the people returned to serving Him. This concept is applicable in our days, even though Passover is a Jewish festival.

In the twenty-first century, we need our leaders to call the people of God to regular repentance. Left to our own devices, we tend to become distracted. We need to seek His face, change from our wicked and selfish ways to allow God to heal our land and bring the prodigals back to Him. This is the hope for future generations, and where better to start than with us! We are thankful for corporate prayer requests made by the Archbishop of Canterbury and Archbishop of York, and look forward to revival and renewal in the Church in the UK.

Heal our nation

Some claim that the era of healing has ended in the Church, however, if people are still being baptised in Christ after experiencing salvation, why should healing in His name end? I do not believe that the Bible indicated the end of ministry gifts before the return of Christ. Instead, He said the power of the Holy Spirit has been released upon us that we might do even greater works than Him, because He conquered sin and death and returned to the Father. He expects more from the Church, because we have time until Christ returns.

I believe that the Church underestimates the divine power at its disposal, lays hold of it too little for healing, and gets distracted by bureaucracy, forsaking the spiritual for fleshly concerns The Church has switched priority, focusing first on the love of humanity ahead of love for the Father. In Matthew 22:37 Jesus said 'Thou shalt love the Lord your God with all thy heart, and with all thy soul, and with all thy mind. This is the first and great commandment. And the second is like unto it, 'Thou shalt love thy neighbour as thyself'. We are to love the Lord our God first, then we can love our neighbours as ourselves. This is because the love for our neighbour does not necessarily lead to the love of God, but in loving God we receive grace to love others too.

As we seek Him daily, His love, passion, concerns, power and compassion rub off on us. In light of this, we need to visit the Lord regularly for a top-up of His presence in our life, through worship, fellowship, quiet times, conferences, church services and bible study. In these settings we learn to listen and follow His instructions. The world is still groaning for the manifestation of the sons and daughters of God. Are we visible? The world is waiting for the Church to demonstrate God's love and show Jesus to His creation.

> 'Because the creature itself also shall be delivered from the bondage of corruption into the glorious liberty of the children of God. For we know that the whole creation groaneth and travaileth in pain together until now. And not only they, but ourselves also, which have the firstfruits of the Spirit, even we ourselves groan within ourselves, waiting for the adoption, the redemption of our body.'
>
> Romans 8:21-23

Role of medicine in healing

I have a science background with a postgraduate qualification in zoonosis (epidemiology). Therefore, I understand the importance of medicine and medication. However, I have personally experienced and do experience healing very frequently in my personal life, and find it cheaper to operate this way. It strengthens my faith and confidence in God's word. Even though healthcare in the UK is relatively free (except for prescription charges for those earning higher salaries), Jehovah has been very gracious to me in enjoying good health, by His grace!

Every time I travel to African countries, I witness people with lots of health challenges. To start with, living in mosquito-infested tropical areas means taking sensible precautions daily to maintain good health. I know that regular studying of the scriptures releases life. Jesus said in John 6:63 'the words that I speak unto you, they are spirit, and they are life'.

As we partake of divine life, we experience His grace, even though we fall ill from time to time because of our mortality. Taking medication does not diminish us in any way, however when we can exercise faith, He promised it shall be unto us according to our faith! Since our faith oscillates and we have strong faith for some things, and less faith for others, there is benefit in seeking praying for healing as well as taking appropriate medication. They do complement each other. When prayer works and healing has taken place, only take holy risks when you have a 'blessed assurance' to do so. If you are sure that you are healed of a problem, it is wise to go for a second opinion to be certain, continuing to take medication if you are in any doubt. Pray like the man in Mark 9:24 who said 'Lord, I believe; help thou mine unbelief'. Christ will not let you down.

Personal lifestyle

Those who know me will probably be aware that I have always struggled with my weight. I strive to be healthy by managing my lifestyle, but I have a sweet tooth and love pastry! Nevertheless, I am content with life since my weight is not a major issue. What does that mean in practical terms? I still need to exercise more, watch what I eat and demonstrate self-control. I do not believe Jesus would be overweight if He lived on the earth today, as self-control was one of the fruits of the spirit in Galatians 5:23. This revelation is for me! I need to remind myself constantly to have an encouraging mindset, to improve my quality of my life, and to be a good mentor for my family without beating myself up when I get things wrong. I appreciate that this may not be a problem for you, because not everyone struggles with food. Many of my friends are better disciplined than me, they eat well and exercise regularly. Why focus on this? To prevent weight-associated illnesses such as diabetes, which are an increasing problem in developing countries where managing and treating the consequences of the disease are expensive. Many towns and cities are full of fast-food restaurants, and we travel everywhere by car. How can we introduce healthy changes at an early age when there are fewer playgrounds and very busy roads? Healthy food can seem too expensive, and children are often addicted to gaming or watching television. However, making early steps could avoid a lifetime of medication and treatment. I pray that we can find time in our busy schedules to develop active lifestyles such as walking which is both healthy and inexpensive, and offers the pleasure of being close to nature where we can meditate and think.

Our lifestyles impact on our health and that of our families. As we celebrate our bodies as His temple; let us use our skills, resources and gifts to take good care of our bodies, families and environment!

Questions to ponder

❖ Do you believe in divine healing?
❖ Do you pray for others to be healed?
❖ Can God heal our land?

A bigi bigi thing Jesus done for me
He bless my mama
He bless my papa
He butter my bread and He sugar my tea
He knack am for Satan
he fall for ground
A bigi bigi thing Jesus done for me

Pigin song – West Africa

CHAPTER 7

Prayer for Revival

> 'And I prayed unto the Lord my God, and made my confession, and said, O Lord, the great and dreadful God, keeping the covenant and mercy to them that love him and to them that keep his commandments. We have sinned and have committed iniquity, and have done wickedly, and have rebelled, even by departing from thy precepts and from thy judgments. Neither have we listened to thy servants the prophets, who spoke in your name to our kings, our princes, and our fathers, and to all the people of the land.'
>
> Daniel 9:4-6

Looking back on my student days, I believe we experienced revival in Nigeria from the late seventies until the early eighties, particularly those of us in secondary and tertiary education. It is not therefore surprising that this era also saw the founding of the many independent charismatic churches in Nigeria. There was a hunger for God and a thirst to see Him move. Higher education institutions provided the platform for a move of the

Spirit and, since students were literate, they were able to read the Bible themselves and start challenging cultural practices and traditional beliefs that were contrary to Christian doctrines. Many disgruntled youths left the established church, particularly where clergy and church leaders were members of masonic lodges and secret societies. Cultural sacrifices to appease gods and goddesses were frowned upon and polygamy or promiscuity openly denounced. I believe it was a 'bottom up' change, fuelled by the Holy Spirit through the Scripture Union (SU) movement that greatly improved access to the Bibles. I learnt from the SU that when we place Bibles in the hands of seekers, the Holy Spirit convicts the world of 'sin, and of righteousness, and of judgement' (John 16:8).

Clash of Faiths

Many African countries became independent in the early sixties and, to the best of my knowledge, Nigeria sent some of its most promising and intelligent students to study abroad from the early forties and fifties in preparation for independence. They returned home and became our national leaders, taking up positions as politicians, university lecturers, civil servants, and business merchants. My parents were part of this highly educated group and, upon their return, they were proud to play their part in leading their young and promising nation. Sadly, in 1967 civil war broke out in Nigeria, as the Eastern state of Biafra fought to become a nation in its own right. Life continued in spite of the many challenges. At this time we resided in northern Nigeria, in a place called Zaria, and my dad was a mechanical engineer with the Nigerian Railways. I was the youngest of three and all I could remember were the high pyramids of groundnuts, one of the main cash crops in the region. After the war ended we moved to Lagos. As a young child, I became aware of attending church every Sunday, except for mum because she was a Muslim. Her parents were Muslims but her uncle became a Catholic priest and she moved to live with him at Ijebu (Western Nigeria) so she could get an education. In her time, Muslim girls did not have to get any education so her sister became a trader just like my grandmother. In fact, my aunt was much better off than my mum, because a trader earned much more than a school teacher.

My mum lived with her uncle during term time and she adopted the name Christine. However, when she returned home during term breaks, she retained her Muslim identity and was called *Shadia.* Being from Western Nigeria, this was common practice. We visited mum's hometown often during holidays, especially during traditional and religious festivals. My grandmother's neighbour at Iperu – Remo, was a traditionalist, and he had lots of visitors come and visit his house during festivals. We enjoyed the celebratory experiences with my cousins. However, my siblings and I were not involved with traditional rituals because my dad, as a Christian, was against it.

More important was the influence of my paternal grandfather, who was an occultist before he encountered Christ and became a born-again Christian and later a Methodist. He forbade any involvement with pagan activities and his love for hymns and scriptures inspired me greatly as a child. My grandfather lived in Oshodi, Lagos, therefore we saw him quite often but did not consider these visits very special because we did not have to travel out of Lagos, whereas visits to my maternal grandparents in Iperu felt like a holiday.

The challenge facing our parents at that time was the difficulty of reconciling traditional cultural practices with Christianity. Most of our grandparents were not literate, and were unable to understand why their gods and traditional beliefs were shunned after their children returned from their studies abroad. Our parents grew up in rural areas and moved to towns and cities when they took up jobs as civil servants or prominent business owners. We children grew up in urban areas and we were literate from childhood, which further removed us from traditional rituals and beliefs. In addition, we had Bibles at our disposal and participated at school assemblies where we learnt hymns and Christian songs. Most of us progressed to boarding grammar or secondary schools. Our young, eager hearts were ready for the things of God, which made it easy to encounter Christ Unbeknown to us, we were ready for a move of the Spirit, as we had been fully exposed to the gospel and this had replaced previous belief systems in our lives. In the words of Psalm 85:6, 'Wilt thou not revive us again: that thy people may rejoice in thee?'

Praying for repentance

As we matured in Christ at boarding school, there was increasing recognition of the need for corporate repentance before Him. This was more evident when students visited relatives in communities where it was common to serve certain deities, or when they returned to live in rural places. Independent churches started springing up as small groups of Christians sought His face for forgiveness, and addressed difficult contextual issues scripturally. These churches offered options for new believers wishing to practise their faith as born-again Christians. These new fellowships and independent churches would often organise gatherings dedicated to fasting and prayer during school term breaks. There would also be prayer vigils and crusades.

> 'Therefore also now, saith the Lord, turn ye even to me with all your heart, and with fasting, and with weeping, and with mourning: And rend your heart, and not your garments, and turn unto the Lord your God: for he is gracious and

merciful, slow to anger, and of great kindness, and repenteth him of the evil.'

Joel 2:12-13

In addition to holiday times, people came together to pray all night, and shared testimonies after the worship sessions regularly on the last Friday night of each month. Gradually the spiritual atmosphere was conducive for a move of the Spirit.

Crusades, evangelistic outreaches, night vigils, corporate fasting and public prayer sessions were uncommon in the traditional big churches, except at Lenten season. In fairness, there was little understanding of how to handle spiritual encounters or deal with traditional spiritualism because the church leaders were not taught these skills at established theological colleges and universities. These denominational churches: Anglican, Methodist, Baptist, etc., struggled to deviate from the liturgies in their prayer books, therefore such spiritual complexities were only addressed by the newer churches.

Strange spiritual encounters

I lived in Lagos during my primary school years, before gaining admission into Queen's School, Ibadan (a girls-only grammar school) at the age of ten, after passing my common entrance examination (similar to the 11+ in the UK). It was a reputable grammar school and I was glad of the opportunity. Most students were admitted based on their academic ability, although a few places were allocated to girls from disadvantaged backgrounds in the state, and rightly so. Many of these girls were from rural areas and began joining the school in 1977, when secondary education became free in Oyo state. I heard from a friend how she was approached by another girl at school. The girl asked her if she wanted to summon a wild bird; she said yes and the wild bird that was hovering came over and perched on her hand. That night when she slept, she said she dreamt and saw herself in a group with other girls. Unbeknown to her, she was given power to cast spells. On another occasion, I remember waking up in the middle of the night and felt a huge weight like an elephant sleeping on my chest. Having heard from someone else what to do, I managed to say 'Jesus', and the weight disappeared. We were perplexed as we had never heard of anything like this before. These were strange and frightening events for young girls like me living in a boarding school. This encounter demonstrated that the name of Jesus was the recommended solution to these inexplicable and unsettling occurrences. I therefore stuck to reading my Bible and calling on His name when needed. There were many ongoing spiritual puzzles, and as always the Bible provided answers:

> 'There shall not be found among you anyone that maketh his son or his daughter pass through the fire, or that useth divination, or an observer of times, or an enchanter, or a witch. Or a charmer, or a consulter with familiar spirits, or a wizard, or a necromancer (one who communicates with the dead). For all that do these things are an abomination unto the Lord:and because of these abominations the Lord thy God doth drive them out from before thee.'
>
> Deuteronomy 18:10-12, explanation in brackets added

Praying for Revival

You may be wondering how all these events pointed to revival, and the answer is that they made us seek the truth and assurance of salvation. Prayers for my generation had started long before my time, and we only joined the momentum. There were people persistently praying for a move of the Spirit in Nigeria that led to many encountering the Messiah. The church woke up from its sleep to take charge, and establish God's kingdom on earth. In my humble opinion; the revival was borne out of love for God and a passion to see His people saved.

> 'For, behold, the darkness shall cover the earth, and gross darkness the people; but the Lord shall arise upon thee, and His glory shall be seen upon thee. And the Gentiles shall come to thy light, and kings to the brightness of thy rising. Lift up thine eyes round about, and see: all they gather themselves together, they come to thee: thy sons shall come from afar, and thy daughters shall be nursed at thy side.'
>
> Isaiah 60:2-4

As revival broke out there was the acknowledgement and confession of sins; particularly addressing the mixture of ungodly practices with the Christian faith, followed by personal and corporate prayers of repentance. We experienced a persistent hunger and thirst for righteousness, and engaged in regular fasting and praying and as we continued to seek His face. There was an emphasis on scriptural living and the scriptures became significant in guiding activities and giving direction. We expected Him to move, and His power was released at gatherings promoting unity of Christians from different churches. Praise and worship were often awesome, with dancing and jubilation. We moved with the rhythm in thanksgiving for the great things He had done. My mum testified that I was dancing right from within her womb and I never disappointed her whilst on the floor. This was the story of many of us. We sang praises and worshipped God at every opportunity, and in every place. When our teacher did not show up for classes, we would spontaneously sing in harmony, beating our desks as drums and praising God until the class period ended. The teacher next door would usually caution us or put an end to it. Perhaps because there was no social media, this was our creative way of amusing ourselves and pleasing our heavenly father too! Our joy and gladness must have pleased Him and probably attracted the ministry of the Holy Spirit regardless of the challenges encountered. Who knows?

Corporate fasting and prayers

Often revival prayers are linked with fasting and these either start with a person or group burdened to pray. Fasting for revival is often more effectively done corporately as recorded in the Bible when He inspired His servants.

Then I proclaimed a fast there at the river of Ahava, that we might afflict ourselves before our God, to seek of him a right way for us and our little ones, and all our substance' (Ezra 8:21). On this occasion, Ezra as leader and scribe, proclaimed a corporate fast to seek God's direction.

Esther asked her people to join her in a fast to seek God's face to overturn the decree that would have annihilated the Jews: 'And in every province wheresoever the king's commandment and his decree came, there was great mourning among the Jews, and fasting and weeping, and wailing and many lay in sackcloth and ashes (Esther 4:3). The fast was personally motivated for **corporate benefit**.

Daniel was seeking God for **revelation** about the future of his nation Israel: 'And I set my face unto the Lord God, to seek by prayer and supplications, with fasting, and sackcloth, and ashes' (Daniel 9:3). This was personal fasting to understand the times and seasons.

Joel, as God's prophet, declared a corporate fast for **repentance**: 'Therefore also now, saith the Lord, turn ye even to me with all your heart, and with fasting, and with weeping, and with mourning' (Joel 2:12). Joel declared a corporate fast to draw the people closer to God.

In Isaiah corporate prayer and fasting was commanded by God as an act of **repentance**: 'Cry aloud, spare not, lift up thy voice like a trumpet, and shew my people their transgression, and the house of Jacob their sins (Isaiah 58:1).

Fasting is not an easy thing to do, so why should we fast, and what kind of attitude should we adopt during fasting? fte Israelites were frustrated because they felt nothing happened during their fast: 'Wherefore have we fasted, they say, and thou seest not? Wherefore have we afflicted our soul, and thou takest no knowledge?' (Isaiah 58:3). God responds by telling Isaiah the reasons for fasting, expected behaviours and desired outcomes.

> 'Is not this the fast I have chosen? To loose the bands of wickedness, to undo the heavy burdens, and to let the oppressed go free, and that ye break every yoke? Is it not to deal thy bread to the hungry, and that thou bring the poor that are cast out to thy house? When thou seest the naked, that thou cover him; and that thou hide not thyself from thine own flesh?'
>
> (Isaiah 58:7).

When we take God's directives on board, we experience the reward of fasting listed in Isaiah 58:

> 'Then shall thy light break forth as the morning, and thine health shall spring forth speedily: and thy righteousness shall go before thee; the glory

> of the Lord shall be your reward. Then thou shall
> call, and the Lord shall answer.'
>
> Isaiah 58:8-9

With the right attitude, we can also enjoy personal and spiritual benefits:

> 'If thou take away from the midst of thee the
> yoke, the putting forth of the finger, and
> speaking vanity; And if thou draw out thy soul
> to the hungry, and satisfy the afflicted soul; then
> shall thy light rise in obscurity, and your darkness
> be as the noon day: And the Lord shall guide
> thee continually, and satisfy thy soul in drought,
> and make fat thy bones: and thou shalt be like
> a watered garden, and like a spring of water,
> whose waters fail not. And they that shall be of
> thee shall build the old waste places: thou shalt
> raise up the foundations of many generations;
> and thou shalt be called, the repairer of the
> breach, the Restorer of paths to dwell in.'
>
> Isaiah 58:9-12

Even though fasting is not an easy feat, its benefits definitely outweigh the sacrifice, and the breakthrough is well worth it! No wonder Christ endorsed regular fasting and praying and, as an example, He also fasted and prayed at the start of His three year ministry. He expects us as His disciples to fast and pray regularly. In Mark 2:18 we note that both the disciples of John and the Pharisees used to fast:

> 'and they come and say unto Him, Why do the
> disciples of John and of the Pharisees fast, but
> your disciples fast not? And Jesus said unto

them, Can the children of the bridechamber
fast, while the bridegroom is with them? As long
as they have the bridegroom with them, they
cannot fast. But the days will come, when the
bridegroom shall be taken away from them, and
then shall they fast in those days.'

Mark 2:18-20

Thankfully this comment was made by Jesus, and it is
evident that other religious practices tap into this truth to reap
the immense benefits of subduing the flesh and strengthening
the spirit.

Ongoing challenge

With hindsight, I realised there was a great emphasis on
personal salvation and holiness but less on social holiness. I
was delighted to know that my holiness was founded on what
Christ did for me, which took much of the burden off me, be
ause I did not have to be bogged down by the traditions of
men. It was liberating to know I was a 'work in progress', being
transformed daily in my faith journey. Objectively, I do not think
the charismatic churches in Nigeria have challenged themselves
over the years to promote social righteousness as described in
Isaiah 58:7. We have many committed Christians in Nigeria but
Christian values are slow in permeating the fabric of our society.
Corporate culture and government practices hardly reflect godly
values as they should, considering that many Nigerians are
people of faith. Could this be because many are not in positions
to effect change, or do we have difficulty separating our personal
values from work? I know many individuals with great values but
have government agencies been challenging societal injustice?
Many born-again Christians are reluctant to get into politics,

so as to preserve their good reputation. That is not to say there are no well-principled Nigerians with good values in politics, irrespective of their faiths. However, time and time again they are subsumed by party politics. Nevertheless, there is hope. In recent years the number of committed Christians in parliament has increased, and I hope and pray that godly values will be championed by Nigerian government leaders and officials as time goes on.

Compounding the situation in Nigeria have been the ongoing terrorist attacks in the north-Eastern states of Borno, Adamawa and Yobe. The church in northern Nigeria has been battered, bruised and persecuted severely. Muslims of these regions have not been exempt and some of their leaders have also been attacked. Christians, as minority groups in these areas, need our prayers and support to remain in this region. Christians in southern Nigeria might be unable to comprehend the challenges faced by Christians in northern Nigeria. I pray that the Church in Nigeria jointly seeks divine counsel, and works with the Nigerian government on how best to handle this situation in order to eliminate terrorism. This will require spiritual, political, economic, technological and social skills in addition to the need for security, intelligence and working in collaboration with neighbouring countries.

I sometimes wonder how things became so bad in northern Nigeria. Was it because the Church took its eyes off Christ as its focus, and became more interested in material things? Was it because the government was too slow to tackle evil perpetrators? Was there an intelligence lapse? Did the country's inability to address poverty and justice aggravate the situation? There are lots of questions; nevertheless, we Christians must support Nigeria with prayers and hope that our government can win the battle against terrorism.

Co-existence of faiths

Interfaith is a sensitive but significant topic within Christian communities in Nigeria, particularly after the Boko Haram insurgencies. However, as Africans, and Nigerians in particular, we need to understand how to coexist peacefully in our communities. As mentioned earlier, my mum and grandparents were Muslims. We should first celebrate ourselves as Nigerians and respect everyone's right to live and dwell in our beloved country irrespective of faith or tribe. No one can claim more rights than anyone else, we are all equal and equally loved by God. Secondly, terrorism does not serve anyone except the perpetrators. Both Muslims and Christians have been badly affected, therefore we should work together and root out these evil perpetrators, and the politicians who are using the situation for their own selfish ambitions. Lastly, both religions expect their followers to be evangelical. We need to acknowledge our differences, respect each other's views and identify areas we could serve humanity together, for example in the arenas of health, the empowerment of women and education.

Followers of each religion should know the pillars of their faiths, and respect everyone's right to choose a faith and defend it peacefully when challenged. As a Christian, I can share what Christ did for me and how He transformed my life, without ridiculing other beliefs. The best I can do after that is to pray and positively influence others.

I can share this because my mother did not convert to Christianity overnight. She had to be positively influenced, evaluate the impact of converting to Christianity and ask relevant questions. I remember once telling her, mum I wish to see you in heaven because Jesus said in John 14: 'And if I go and prepare a place for you, I will come again, and receive you unto myself; that where I am, there ye may be also'. (John 14:3). Jesus was certain about our final destination, and He gave us a free pass to heaven when he paid the price with his life. Moreover, he came down to earth from heaven so he was succinct in his descriptions of heaven, and was not guessing; there will be mansions, angels, elders, other saints, etc. Furthermore, there will be praise and worship, and we will be participants. What more could we want? We do not need to miss out on this wonderful experience, as it goes on and on, with no 'night-time' because the Lamb of God radiates light:

> 'And there shall be no night there; and they need no candle, neither light of the sun, for the Lord God gives them light: and they shall reign forever and ever.'
>
> Revelation 22:5

I explained to my mum, that this picture of heaven was not guess work, and that she could access heaven by grace. She did not have to worry about insufficient good works, or depend on 'Inshallah' (i.e. if God wills). And the good news does not end there, we shall judge the angels and reign with Him when He comes for us. What a wonderful promise!

> 'Know ye not that we shall judge angels? How much more, things that pertain to this life?'
>
> 1 Corinthians 6:3

In the meantime, many celebrations take place in heaven when sinners repent and follow Jesus: 'Likewise I say unto you, there is joy in the presence of the angels of God over one sinner who repenteth.' Luke 15:10. I told my mum that she had nothing to lose by coming to His camp, because Jesus exchanges your condemnation for His justification! In the end, we all become royalty and reign with Him! It took my mum over thirty years to make the decision to be a follower of Christ, and I was glad she eventually did. What does that tell me? Only that the Spirit of God convicts men and women of sin. We just need to love and pray for people, living out lives transformed by Christ and seeking peace and justice for all. Most of all, we must share the love of Christ in a friendly and sensitive way. I pray that as the Nigerian Church continues to address difficult evolving issues, it will tap into His grace for solutions. May His Church be revived, to become His representative on earth, with authority and power!

Questions to ponder

- ❖ Have you ever encountered a clash between faith and culture?
- ❖ What would you do if faced with strange spiritual encounters?
- ❖ What modern issues do we need to tackle as the body of Christ?

London, England

CHAPTER 8

Spiritual Warfare

'For we wrestle not against flesh and blood, but against principalities, against powers, against the rulers of the darkness of this world, against spiritual wickedness in high places.'

Ephesians 6:12

I once heard someone say that there was no evil and perhaps no hell. I smiled and my first thought was, do you read your Bible at all? No one spoke more about hell than Jesus and He persistently reassured us that hell was not intended for us, but made for the devil. However, if one does not accept the price of sin paid by His death on the cross as the sinless Saviour, our salvation is not guaranteed.

I smiled at my friend who said there was no evil in this world. I thought what a wonderful heritage you have in Europe, centuries of Christian values, prayers from generation to generation. The laws and the social fabric were guided by Christian values despite being secularised in recent decades. Centuries of godliness still influence Western Europe and there are remnants of committed

Christians still upholding it in prayer. How long will it last? Hopefully until He returns.

I thought to myself that things might have been different if western countries had experienced centuries of idolatrous practices due to ignorance. Fear, selfishness and oppression pervade society in the absence of the fear of God. Serving lesser gods offers the devil an opportunity to reign, and he takes advantage of ignorance and rules with fear. Satan steals, kills and destroys.

Africa was blessed to have hosted Christ as a baby when his parents were refugees in Egypt before returning to Nazareth. Thank God Christianity still exists in Egypt, and in patches of northern Africa, in spite of the terrible persecutions of Christians.

Christianity came to West Africa following the release of freed slaves on the high seas on the way to America, and many settled in Freetown, Sierra Leone. Eventually on 24 September 1842, Christianity reached the shores of Western Nigeria through Badagry, and it later spread inland to Abeokuta by the return of freed slaves and conversion of the locals (MILUM 1893).

Rev Thomas Freeman and two Ghanaian Methodist couples first brought Christianity to Nigeria. Islam came through northern Nigeria by Saharan traders influenced by the Ottoman Empire in North Africa. Prior to this, traditional beliefs were the order of the day and the custodians ensured the rites and rituals were performed as and when required. Now that Christianity has spread across the nation, one might think that the previous religious and spiritual practices would have disappeared. However, the custodians of the old rituals were not willing to relinquish influence and power as Christianity spread and, problems arise when the two cultures clash.

Evangelistic outreaches

It is difficult to find out much about the social challenges being faced by communities until you attend an evangelistic outreach in that area. Many people bring their problems to such events since counselling centres are very few and far between in West Africa, and the financial pressures of caring for peoples' psychological, emotional and spiritual problems are hugely challenging. Truly, the gospel is the hope of our nation, especially when lives are transformed by healing and deliverance. Such stories in the gospels proved that, as humans, we are both flesh and spirit, with souls that inhabit bodies. These are not myths, but realities as people encounter the power of the cross that saves from sin, sickness and shame. Paul says in Romans 1

> 'For I am not ashamed of the gospel of Christ: for it is the power of God unto salvation to everyone that believeth; to the Jew first, and also to the Greek.'
>
> Romans 1:16

The location of evangelistic outreach influences the problems and spiritual challenges faced by Christian leaders and prayer warriors, because different spiritual forces operate in certain localities. The spiritual effects of idolatry seem to be less acute in urban areas, due to the population being generally better informed and more multicultural. Improved standards of literacy in towns and cities combat superstitious beliefs, and there are more Christians, due to a higher density of churches. However, when evangelistic outreach takes place in rural areas it is an entirely different matter. You must be confident as a child of God and know your authority in Christ! The occultists and witch doctors would take any opportunity to attack or arrest you spiritually, to test your faith. In fact, some daring witch doctors may challenge you openly, because you are invading their territory. Remember, when you leave they remain, therefore it is important to ensure there is a comprehensive follow-up plan for new converts, and prayer teams to uphold good over evil. One does not need to be fearful, but do not underestimate the enemy, and come prepared. As we read in Daniel 11:32: 'But the people that know their God shall be strong, and do exploits.'

Preparations for rural evangelistic outreaches require lots of scriptural prayers ahead of time, to make them successful. Environmental challenges such as heavy rains throughout the event are possible in the open air. Lack of reliable power supply, malfunctioning generators, very low turnout, lack of miracles, key participants falling ill just before the crusade, car accidents on the way to the venue, and so on, can create obstacles. So, how did renowned evangelists like the late Archbishop Benson Idahosa, Pastor Reinhardt Bonke, Bishop David Oyedepo, Pastor Adeboye, and Reverend Wale Oke handle their outreaches successfully and enjoy triumphant ministries? They had to prepare spiritually, physically and financially!

They all had teams of intercessors like forerunners. What do I mean by that? In many Western countries, intercessory prayers could be about praying for countries and people in difficulties, those encountering persecution, for example, or involving natural disasters. This is often included in the liturgy or in corporate prayers during a meeting. However, in the charismatic and Pentecostal circles, intercessory prayer is also about standing in the gap spiritually until a believer becomes a disciple, or conversion ensues. They pray for the mercy of God, by the power of the Holy Spirit, and build up their faith by staying in God's love for guidance and protection.

> 'But ye, beloved, building up yourselves on your
> most holy faith, praying in the Holy Ghost, keep

yourselves in the love of God, looking for the
mercy of our Lord Jesus Christ unto eternal life.'
Jude1:20-21

Only when we are well soaked in and surrounded by His Spirit
are we ready for spiritual warfare, knowing that our opponents
have dwelt in these territories much longer, and would try to
upset our strategy by hindering the establishment or expansion
of Christ's kingdom.

Taking over kingdoms territories

Intercessors start prayers at least a week or more prior
to crusades, particularly if thousands are expected to attend.
They are there to scan the spiritual environment and claim the
territory in prayer. As indicated in Jeremiah 1:10, intercessors
declare the Lordship of Jesus through prayers, by rooting out,
pulling down, destroying and throwing down evil practices and
beliefs in His name. Afterwards the Holy Spirit is invited to build
and to plant, establishing God's kingdom in the territory.

Handling strongholds

Pulling down strongholds means challenging long-standing
traditions that extol local deities, for example 'Ogun' the god of
Iron, 'Yemoja' the fertility goddess and 'Oshun' the love goddess.
These deities have been worshipped and offered sacrifices by
worshippers down through the ages. The demonic influence
of spirits is most entrenched where the deity is a tribal god or
goddess, with its priests and regular rituals. Spiritual warfare is
about setting people free from fear and bondage to follow Jesus
as Lord and Saviour. In addition, conscious and unconscious

covenants made on their behalf need to be broken. In some cases, generational bonds were made on behalf of clans, families and communities and such links must be broken by praying in the name of Jesus.

> 'For though we walk in the flesh, we do not war after the flesh: For the weapons of our warfare are not carnal but mighty through God to the pulling down of strongholds.'
>
> 2 Corinthians 10:3-4

Setting the captives free

As mentioned earlier, deliverance ministry is a core part of evangelism in rural areas, where no church has been planted. Luke 4:18 encapsulates Jesus' manifesto and mentions a number of the challenges of physical and spiritual deliverance encountered when sharing the gospel.

> 'The Spirit of the Lord is upon me, because He hath anointed me to preach the gospel to the **poor**; He has sent me to heal the **brokenhearted**, to preach liberty to the **captives**, and recovering of sight to the **blind**, to set at liberty them that are **bruised**.'
>
> Luke 4:18

Deliverance ministry, especially in Africa, is not limited to evangelistic outreaches, but requires sustained counselling, support, guidance, empowerment, advocacy, love and prayers. No wonder intercession is so rewarding, especially when one witnesses people liberated and lives and communities transformed as we pray in the name of Jesus.

Follow- up

Intercessors do not only play the forerunner, but also follow up after the main event. New converts need to be upheld in prayer until they become established disciples. Remember, evangelists leave after outreaches and crusades but converts remain in their communities and families and need the skills, knowledge and guidance to lead a Christian lifestyle, read scripture, manage the temptations of returning to familiar ways, endure persecutions, develop a prayer life and become part of a Christian fellowship.

> 'Epaphras, who is one of you, a servant of Christ, saluteth you, always labouring fervently for you in prayers, that ye may stand perfect and complete in all the will of God.'
>
> Colossians 4:12

Spiritual warfare is necessary and significant in advancing God's kingdom on earth. Of course spiritual attacks are likely, in the same way that any combatant can expect to be attacked on the battlefield. Fear not, for He has the won the battle against Satan and given us the victory. We just need to plug into His victory as we journey through life:

> 'And having spoiled principalities and powers, he made a shew of them openly, triumphing over them in it.'
>
> Colossian 2:15

Casting out demons

This is not a popular topic in the West, even though Jesus was known to cast out many demons, as did His disciples and Paul after His death. The great commission mentions this in Mark:

> 'And these signs shall follow them that believe;
> in my name shall they cast out devils; they shall
> speak with new tongues;'
>
> Mark 16:17

Why cast out demons in our day? I believe it is because demons still oppress, suppress and possess people; inflicting pain and havoc in their lives and communities.

Demons may also manifest during rituals, festivals or when cast out using the authority of the name of Jesus. Whenever casting out of demons takes place, one should speak directly to the possessed person: 'IN THE NAME OF JESUS, I cast you out. Do not return to this domain or person!' This is to ensure that the demons do not return into the person, as Jesus remarked below. However, not all demons do return to their victims; some go elsewhere, as was the case of the Gadarenes man in Luke 8 when the demons went into nearby pigs.

> 'When the unclean spirit is gone out of a man,
> he walketh through dry places, seeking rest, and
> findeth none. Then he saith, 'I will return into my
> house from whence I came out'; and when he is
> come, he findeth it empty, swept, and garnished.
> Then goeth he, and taketh with himself seven
> other spirits more wicked than himself, and they
> enter in and dwell there: and the last state of that
> man is worse than the first.'
>
> Matthew 12:43-45

Why call on the name of Jesus? Because the Bible informs us: 'That at the name of Jesus every knee should bow, of things in heaven, and of things on earth, and of things under the earth' (Philippians 2:10). It is **the name** that gives the victory, not how articulate our prayers sound. Sometimes, the demon will manifest even after ordering it out. Take no notice of the tantrums or distractions. Do not get into any debate or discussion but do ensure that the person being delivered is in a safe environment, to avoid getting physically hurt.

> 'And when they were come to the multitude, there came to Him a certain man, kneeling down to him, and saying, 'Lord, have mercy on my son: for he is lunatic, and sore vexed: for often times he **falleth into the fire**, and **often into the water**. And I brought him to thy disciples, and they could not cure him. Then Jesus answered and said, O faithless and perverse generation, how long shall I be with you? How long shall I suffer you? Bring him hither to me. And Jesus rebuked the devil; and he departed out of him: and the child was cured from that very hour.'
> Matthew 17:14-18

In Matthew 28:18, Jesus assured us that all power has been given to Him and He demonstrated it in this passage above. Therefore we should have faith to cast out demons.

Another weapon at our disposal is appropriating the blood of the Lamb of God as protection as the Israelites applied the blood of the Passover lamb. Is this biblical? Let us check the Bible.

> 'Then Moses called for all the elders of Israel, and said unto them, Draw out and take you a lamb according to your families, and kill the Passover.

> And ye shall take a bunch of hyssop, and dip
> it in the blood that is in the bason (basin) and
> strike the lintel and the two side posts with the
> blood that is in the bason (basin); and none of
> you shall go out at the door of his house until the
> morning. For the Lord will pass through to smite
> the Egyptians; and when he seeth the blood
> upon the lintel, and on the two side posts, the
> Lord will pass over the door, and will not suffer
> the destroyer to come in unto your houses to
> smite you.'
>
> Exodus 12: 21-23 (explanation in brackets)

'The next day, John seeth Jesus coming unto him, and saith, Behold the Lamb of God, which taketh away the sin of the world.' John 1:29

I remember once praying for a female colleague who frequently had nightmares and, saw masquerades (visions of masked ancestors) pursuing her in her dreams. I prayed for her and, she was delivered; no more nightmares. However another team member present during the deliverance session, hesitantly shared later that he too had started seeing 'masquerades' (masked ancestors) in his dreams after the event. I prayed for him and it stopped. Then I realised that spiritual maturity differs, due to varying levels of faith; even though we can all cast out demons.

> 'Then He called his twelve disciples together, and
> gave them power and authority over all devils,
> and to cure diseases.'
>
> Luke 9:1

Jesus did not limit this authority to the twelve disciples – He gave power and authority to the seventy followers too, giving them power to 'tread on serpents and scorpions, and over all the power of the enemy: and nothing shall by any means hurt you,' Luke 10:19. Demons are the devil's associates seeking to do his will, and wreak havoc, but Jesus came to give us life in abundance.

In these texts, they are called devils. Afflictions caused by devils or demons are not always obvious. Often, they manifest when threatened or challenged or at an event w ere Jesus is being glorified. Demons can manifest at special Christian gatherings where God's anointing is present to heal and deliver even without any direct interaction. They become uneasy in His presence, as demonstrated by the possessed man who lived in tombs until he encountered Jesus and was delivered.

> 'And they arrived at the country of the Gadarenes, which is over against Galilee. And when he went forth to land, there met him out of the city a certain man, which had devils long time, and ware (wore) no clothes, neither abode in any house, but in the tombs. When he saw Jesus, he cried out, and fell down before him, and with a loud voice said, 'What have I to do with thee, Jesus, thou Son of God most high?' I beseech you, torment me not'. (For He had commanded the unclean spirit to come out of the man. For oftentimes it had caught him: and he was kept bound with chains and in fetters; and he brake the bands, and was driven of the devil into the wilderness).'
>
> Luke 8:26-30

I wish to reiterate at this stage that the casting out of demons should be done only when the person is willing to be helped, or the person's parent or guardian requests help, to ensure that the

Spiritual Warfare

end state is not worse than the beginning. Before conducting deliverance, know your authority in Christ and don't fake it! The unclean spirits know your level of faith and can differentiate performance from faith.

> 'And the evil spirit answered and said, 'Jesus I know, and Paul I know; but who are ye?' And the man in whom the evil spirit was leaped on them, overpowered them, and prevailed against them, so that they fled out of that house naked and wounded.'
>
> Acts 19:15-16

If you feel a check in your spirit before casting out the demon, delay the prayer and seek help from other mature believers like the disciples did in the New Testament. It might mean you need to fast and pray to discern how best to deal with the situation or how to strengthen your faith.

Fasting and prayer

A word of caution, casting out demons is not always predictable, therefore be prepared spiritually and mentally. There could be some antics by the demon such as frothing at the mouth, bad language, shrieking or shouting. Many servants of God try to fast and pray before attending evangelical events to increase their spiritual sensitivity and discern what the Spirit is saying. Nonetheless, just do your best, and leave the rest to God. I do not personally go looking for those in need of deliverance, probably because it is not my main ministry. Probably someone else's.

I remember attending a church at Witney, in Oxfordshire in 2008-09. There was a lovely lady that usually sat the back.

On several occasions, whenever it was worship time, she would suddenly become very noisy, disrupting the service and distracting everyone. This happened with regularity and the church leaders did not know what to do. Immediately after service, she became normal again and it was clear that she was not fully in control of herself. The church leader approached me and asked if I could help.

We jointly agreed a date and I arranged a short prayer of deliverance with the woman, which was successful, because the next time she came to church she remained normal throughout the service. However, I cautioned her about what she was exposing herself to, e.g. spiritualists, new age practices, casting spells, etc, and how her spirit could be affected by what she watched, read, or where she visited. The incident could also have been due to generational ties or past involvement in activities such as palm reading, necromancy, etc, which are best avoided. Whatever it was, she was delivered in Jesus' name.

Questions to ponder

- ❖ Have you ever encountered spiritual warfare?
- ❖ How do I help my friend who is dabbling in non-Christian rituals and beliefs?
- ❖ I wish to go on mission trips abroad, how do I prepare?

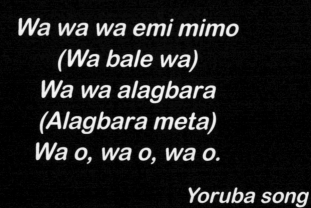

CHAPTER 9

Deliver us from Evil

'After this manner therefore pray ye: Our Father
which art in heaven, Hallowed be Thy name. Thy
kingdom come. Thy will be done in earth, as it is
in heaven. Give us this day our daily bread. And
forgive us our debts, as we forgive our debtors.
And lead us not into temptation, but deliver
us from evil: For Thine is the kingdom, and the
power, and the glory, forever. Amen.'

Matthew 6:9-13

I enjoy having fun, so delving into wrestling with spiritual
wickedness is hard work! Nonetheless, having discussed the
presence of evil in the previous chapter, it is only proper to
mention how to equip ourselves against the enemy. This is a
delicate topic, therefore I do not go snooping around for the
devil or seeking out what he is doing. But if he attacks, or tries
to disrupt God's will, or afflicts someone seeking help, then God
expects us to be ready to intervene through Christ. 'Be sober,
be vigilant; because your adversary the devil as a roaring lion,
walketh about, seeking whom he may devour' (1 Peter 5:8-11).

It is the devil who loiters about, nevertheless, light always overcomes darkness. As ambassadors of Christ, we should shine and exude Jesus, because His love and power overcomes the devil. We sometimes have to engage him using the power and authority of Christ: 'For the kingdom of God is not in word but in power.'(1 Corinthians 4:20).

Intercession ~ 1 John 3:16

John 3:16 is a popular scripture we can all recite: 'For God so loved the world ...' a summary of how God loves us so much that He gave us His best, 'and whosoever believes in Him shall have eternal life'. This passage also admonishes us that if we have tasted this sacrificial love, we should be willing to serve others too as a sign of our Christian maturity. By this, we know that He laid down his life for us, and we ought to lay down our lives for our friends. I believe intercession is about standing in the gap and promoting mediation between God and humanity as Jesus did for us, and Abraham did for the people of Sodom and Gomorrah.

> 'And he said, 'Behold now, I have taken upon me to speak unto the Lord: peradventure there shall be twenty found there'. And He said, 'I will not destroy it for twenty's sake'. And he said, Oh let not the Lord be angry, and I will speak yet but this once: peradventure ten shall be found there. And He said, 'I will not destroy it for ten's sake'. And the Lord went his way, as soon as he had left communing with Abraham: and Abraham returned unto his place.'
>
> Genesis 18:31

Intercession is not a glamorous ministry, and it requires patience and commitment because the results are not quickly evident. Those being interceded for, are often unaware of your being interceded for are often unaware of your prayers, as in the case of Abraham pleading with God to avert destruction from Sodom in Genesis 18. Though hidden, it is a powerful ministry that gains His attention, requesting mercy instead of judgement, compassion and deliverance from evil. Intercessory prayers could be for people encountering unpleasant occurrences.

> 'And now I come to thee; and these things I speak in the world, that they might have my joy fulfilled in themselves. I have given them thy word; and the world has hated them, because they are not of the world, even as I am not of the world. I pray not that thou shouldest take them out of the world, but that you shouldest keep them from the evil.'
>
> John 17:13-15

We empathise with those in difficulty, request breakthrough in the face of problems, peace to replace conflict and we intercede for a change of heart of the reb llious. However, intercession can go beyond this, by declaring prophetic prayers to avert evil, demolishing spiritual wickedness in order to plant His kingdom on earth as it is in heaven. To achieve this, we need His inspiration and the power of the Holy Spirit.

> 'It is Christ that died, yea rather, that is risen again, who is even at the right hand of God, who also maketh intercession for us.'
>
> Romans 8:34

Christ prays for us, and urges us to pray for one another. However, there are times when we do not know what to pray for.

'Likewise the Spirit also helps in our infirmities: for we know not what we should pray for as we ought: but the Spirit Himself maketh intercession for us with groaning which cannot be uttered. And He that searcheth the hearts knoweth what is the mind of the Spirit, because He maketh intercession for the saints according to the will of God.'

Romans 8:26-28

At such times, we call on the Holy Spirit to help us.

Equipping ourselves

How then can we equip ourselves? By putting on the whole armour of God, as described in Ephesians 6:10-18. This is a package of protective tools received by all believers in Christ. We become more skilful in the use of these tools as we mature in Christ, praying always with all prayers and supplication in the spirit, using the shield of faith to ward off attacks from the evil one, and wielding His word offensively as the Sword of the Spirit against the devil and his schemes. Our ultimate goal is to be victorious like Jesus:

'Again, the devil taketh him up into an exceeding high mountain, and sheweth him all the kingdoms of the world, and the glory of them; and saith unto him, 'All these things will I give thee, if thou wilt fall down and worship me'. Then saith Jesus unto him, 'Get thee hence, Satan: for it is written, thou shalt worship the Lord thy God, and him only shalt thou serve'. Then the

devil leaveth him, and, behold, angels came and
ministered unto him.'

Matthew 4:8-11

As an intercessor, another much-needed attribute is the
ability to hear God. You could say that this is obvious as a Christian,
however it helps in knowing how to direct your prayers and what
spiritual activities in which to engage. I remember my pastor at
Ulster Temple in Belfast sharing how he prayed for an intercessor
to come to his church. He attended a Christian leadership
Conference at Bradford in England and was told to pray for an
African intercessor because they could prevail in prayer. His reply
was, 'Who would come to Belfast, when everyone was leaving?'
However, when he returned home, he was so desperate he fell on
his knees alone at home, praying for an African intercessor. A few
months later, I walked into the church with two young children.
I was the first and (at that time) only African in the church. (I will
share about my mission call in a future chapter). Upon my arrival,
he realised his request had been granted.

Scanning the spiritual environment

So, I had just moved into a new city, and I had many questions
going round my head like shooting up a spiritual antenna to
assess and understand a new spiritual environment. Apart from
handling the mundane, I had to listen to what was being said
and not said by individuals, and various groups, in the media, at
public places, at schools, and at church. Often I asked the Lord,
about the priorities requiring urgent attention, and how to go
about tackling issues in prayer. In the case of Northern Ireland, I
perceived the Spirit telling me to pray against intransigence and
sectarianism. I was pleading the blood of Jesus as I walked around
in the city, asking that mercy would triumph over judgement,

because the blood of the innocents of the country (like the blood of Abel) was calling for vengeance. Human blood is very powerful and vocal and it takes the blood of Jesus to quieten it, by evoking forgiveness and mercy: 'And to Jesus the mediator of the new covenant, and to the blood of sprinkling,that speaketh better things than that of Abel (Hebrews 12:24).' This exercise took several years, and many had to join in to make spiritual impact in the heavenly places.

Bind the strong man

After discerning what to pray for, I was led to pray in the Spirit to 'bind the strong man'. For Jesus said in Mark 3:27, 'No man can enter into a strong man's house, and spoil his goods, except he will first bind the strong man; and then he will spoil his house. 'This was simply to arrest the devil's activities and then subject men to the rule of Christ. He said in Matthew18:18, 'Verily I say unto you, Whatsoever ye shall bind on earth shall be bound in heaven: and whatsoever ye shall loose on earth shall be loosed in heaven.' This scripture tells us how to stop the chaos caused by demonic forces hindering the spread of the gospel. After binding the strong man in prayers, we pray for the free move of the Holy Spirit and for the lordship of Christ. As we declare Jesus as Lord and proclaim His words, angelic activity increases and we gradually exert authority in heaven, to bring about positive change and move in His will.

Spiritual activities during prayers

This principle was demonstrated in the Bible, and still applies in the twentieth century. Let us evaluate the book of Daniel 9:19.

'O Lord, hear; O Lord, forgive; O Lord, hearken and do; defer not, for thine own sake, O my God: for your city and your people are called by your name. And whiles I was speaking, and praying, and confessing my sin and the sin of my people Israel, and presenting my supplication before the Lord my God for the holy mountain of my God; Yea, whiles I was speaking in prayer, even the man Gabriel, whom I had seen in the vision at the beginning, being caused to fly swiftly, touched me about the time of the evening oblation (prayers).

Daniel 9:19-21, in brackets added

In this instance Daniel was praying when the Archangel Gabriel visited him to explain his vision in response to prayer. Later, Daniel fasted and prayed, in chapter 10 verse 3, and subsequently received another revelation:

'Then said he unto me, Fear not, Daniel: for from the first day thou didst set thine heart to understand, and to chasten thyself before thy God, thy words were heard, and I am come for thy words. But the prince of the kingdom of Persia withstood me for one and twenty days: but, lo, Michael, one of the chief princes, came to help me; and I remained there with the kings of Persia. Now I am come to make thee understand what shall befall thy people in the latter days: for yet the vision is for many days.'

Daniel 10:12-14

This passage of scripture tells us that Daniel's prayers were hampered for twenty-one days until the Archangel Michael came to help Archangel Gabriel overcome the prince of Persia in spiritual warfare. The passage also confirms that Daniel's **words** and **persistence** energised angelic activity until there was a breakthrough. The angels responded to words spoken in prayer and so it is today! As we persistently declare the word, we influence spiritual activity and engagement over our communities, towns, cities and nations. We slowly strengthen good over evil, hope over despair, obedience over disobedience, unity over discord, belief over unbelief and love over hatred. The results of prayer breakthroughs could be visions of things to happen in the future, or explanations of things that had happened in the past to better equip us, as we see with Daniel.

Looking back on my time in Northern Ireland, where I lived for twelve years, I can testify to the gradual change in the spiritual atmosphere over time due to the prayers of the saints. There was an intentional desire to see an end to sectarianism, and increased unity among Christians and their leaders. We participated in Global days of prayer, prayer walks at Stormont, the seat of the Ulster parliament, and began to see increased integration across communities and in primary schools. These changes began to chip away at entrenched sectarianism, and the political establishment slowly moved to reflect this new reality.

Obviously this did not happen overnight. I was there when President Clinton addressed the people, calling for tolerance, and when the Rev. Ian Paisley of the Democratic Unionist Party declared 'no surrender' during one of the Orange marches in Belfast. Nevertheless, years later this honourable elder spokesman shared power with Martin McGinnis of Sinn Fein, which was a miracle that only prayers could bring about. Things were not perfect, but they were much improve by the time I left in 2007. Rev. Ian Paisley died in September 2014 and Martin McGinnis died in March 2017 and I expect intercessory prayers to rise up again to positively influence spiritual engagement in Northern Ireland as the political situation is disrupted once more.

Such challenges are not limited to Northern Ireland. Nigeria was relatively peaceful socially and politically until the late nineties. When I lived in Minna, northern Nigeria, we could pray and preach openly in most parts of the country. The church was growing and things were so peaceful that we may have become distracted with worldly things. Lack of awareness, and lack of education in the general population coupled with the relaxed attitude of our government meant we were unprepared for a spate of terrorist attacks by Boko Haram. Fortunately, our spiritual antennae helped us understand the spiritual activity around us, and we implemented appropriate strategies of prayer and intercession to come against the evil forces in Jesus' name. So, can prayers or spiritual awareness deter such attacks? My view is that prayer heightens our sensitivity to God and His Holy Spirit and this may help uncover the evil plans of the enemy seeking to steal, kill and destroy, as mentioned in the book of John.

> 'The thief cometh not, but for to steal, and to kill, and to destroy: I am come that they might have life, and that they might have it more abundantly.'
>
> John 10:10

There was a time in the distant past when the Syrian army was planning to conquer Israel, and Elisha was able to inform the King of Israel how to avert such plans:

> 'Then the king of Syria warred against Israel, and took counsel with his servants, saying, 'In such and such a place shall be my camp'. And the man of God sent unto the king of Israel, saying, 'Beware that thou pass not such a place; for thither the Syrians are come down'. And the king

of Israel sent to the place which the man of God told him and warned him of, and saved himself there, not once nor twice. therefore the heart of the king of Syria was sore troubled for this thing; and he called his servants, and said unto them, 'Will you not shew me which of us is for the king of Israel?' And one of his servants said, 'None, my lord, O king: but Elisha, the prophet that is in Israel, telleth the king of Israel the words that thou speakest in thy bedchamber.'

2 Kings 6:8-12

I pray for the police and intelligence services around the world to be positively influenced by the Holy Spirit to uncover the evil plans of murder and destruction of human life. May we, as the body of Christ, be able to discern and warn against evil plans like Elijah in our times as we seek to speak peace, tolerance and hope in our communities?

Taking authority over contrary spirits

Spiritual warfare is an ongoing battle with evil, and it has no geographical boundaries. The discernment of prevalent spiritual activities helps intercessors to plan their prayer strategies. We must be bold to promptly pray against, and refuse, any practices that promote unbelief, such as New Age beliefs, spiritism, and sorcery; no matter how benignly they are presented.

Praying becomes increasingly difficult when idolatry and other practices cast spiritual darkness over the people. The opposite is true when there are lots of prayers, and God's light is shining into situations. For example, I visited a Protestant monastery in Mariensee, Germany, where prayers had been said for more than 800 years, predating the Reformation. It was an open monastery, and during my one week retreat there was a blissful spiritual environment due to the amount of prayer taking place. On the other hand, when I first arrived in Oxford in 2007, I was shocked at the level of idolatry. There were many New Age influences and, for the first time, I saw various religious temples and a mosque, plus all kinds of spiritism including Wiccan practices. Many of these influences were considered locally to be 'cultural'. They did not support the supremacy of Christ and, worst of all, there was a widespread spirit of unbelief. I was later thankful for Christian gatherings seeking to enthrone Christ, that His light would shine through against the darkness.

> 'Arise, shine; for thy light is come, and the glory of the Lord is risen upon thee. For, behold, the darkness shall cover the earth, and gross darkness the people: but the Lord shall arise upon thee, and his glory shall be seen upon thee.'
>
> Isaiah 60:1-2

I regard intercession as a 'back-office' operation. It may not be visible, but it is an essential factor for success. However, as we work to destabilise Satan's kingdom through prayer, we are also open to attacks. This emphasises the significance of putting on the whole armour of God. What does that mean? This could be likened to soldiers in war zones. Soldiers wear bulletproof vests, belts holding firearms, helmets, sturdy footwear plus telecommunication equipment. In a similar way, the Bible instructs Christians to put on the whole armour of God for protection and to attack the enemy as described in Ephesians 6: 10-18.

Another way we protect ourselves from Satan is to appropriate the blood of the Jesus – the Lamb of God who takes away the sins of the world. In Exodus chapter 12, God instituted the Passover to protect the Israelites from the 'destroyer' by instructing them to apply the 'blood of a lamb' on the door posts and lintels of the houses in Egypt. They were protected from death but the Egyptians were not. In the same vein, we spiritually apply the blood of Jesus (as it were) on ourselves (spiritual houses) to defend us from spiritual attacks. In addition, we also partake of Holy Communion to shield us from sickness, arguments, emotional turmoil within ourselves and attacks from without. We then become 'more than conquerors' in Christ, as we dwell under the shadow of the Almighty, because we cannot do this on our own. The enemy seeks to lure us away from Christ, and wear us out with unrelenting issues presented by human life. We must choose to keep our gaze on our Saviour, the author and finisher of our faith, irrespective of what we go through, or the victories we enjoy.

Intercession brings us close to God by tuning our spiritual ears to the 'heavenly radio' for regular updates. We are refreshed by His Spirit as we join the elders and angels in heaven, who are praising and worshiping our King. It is exciting to work with His angels who excel in strength and heed the sound of God's words in our mouth, causing changes in the spiritual landscape, as indicated in Psalm 103:

> 'The Lord hath prepared His throne in the Heavens; and His kingdom ruleth over all. Bless the Lord, ye His angels, that excel in strength, that do His commandments, hearkening unto the voice of His word. Bless ye the Lord, all His hosts; ye ministers of His, that do His pleasure. Bless the Lord, all His works in all places of His dominion: bless the Lord, O my soul.'
>
> Psalm 103:19-22

I hope we can spend some time with God in intercession when we set time aside.

Questions to ponder

❖ Does evil exist?
❖ Would I consider becoming an intercessor?
❖ How often am I able to set time aside to be with God?

Lagos - Nigeria

CHAPTER 10

Receive Spiritual Gifts

'And it came to pass, that, while Apollos was at Corinth, Paul having passed through the upper coasts came to Ephesus: and finding certain disciples, He said unto them, 'Have ye received the Holy Ghost since ye believed?' And they said unto him, 'We have not so much as heard whether there be any Holy Ghost.' And he said unto them, 'Unto what then were ye baptized?' And they said, 'Unto John's baptism.' Then said Paul, 'John verily baptized with the baptism of repentance, saying unto the people, that they should believe on him which should come after him, that is, in Christ Jesus.' When they heard this, they were baptized in the name of the Lord Jesus.'

Acts 19:1-5

In my opinion, the best gift the English gave to the world was the Bible, and they should be very proud of it! There have been many translations of portions of the Bible into English; however, some literature attributes the first handwritten version of the full Bible translated from Hebrew and Greek texts to John Wycliffe, an Oxford professor, scholar and theologian in 1380 Prior to this, the Bible was written in Latin. The first printed English Bible, the Tyndale Bible, was said to have been in 1526. The English Bible was eventually mass-produced, and I am honoured and privileged to sit on the Board of Trustees of the Bible Society. The vision of the Bible Society is to encourage the wider circulation and use of the Bible, and I am wholeheartedly committed to this goal, since the Bible transformed my life!

At my university campus in Ibadan, we read the Bible and discussed various issues important to us together in each other's rooms in student accommodation, mostly at weekends. I remember us discussing the baptism of the Holy Spirit, wondering whether it still happens, and whether we could experience it? We also wondered how we would know that we had received the Holy Spirit and not another undesirable spirit? Then we debated and cross-referenced the Bible. Finally, we agreed with this passage of scripture:

> 'And I say unto you, Ask and it shall be given you; seek, and ye shall find; knock, and it shall be opened unto you. For every one that asketh receiveth; and he that seeketh findeth; and to him that knocketh it shall be opened. If a son shall ask bread of any of you that is a father, will he give him a stone? Or if he ask a fish, will he for a fish give him a serpent? Or if he shall ask an egg, will he offer him a scorpion? If ye then, being evil, know how to give good gifts unto your

children: how much more shall your heavenly
Father give the Holy Spirit to them that ask him?'
Luke 11:9-13

This passage was music to our ears because the statement
was made by Jesus, not His disciples. We were excited and full of
expectation because the Acts of the Apostles were to become
real to us. We truly believed God's words. That Friday evening,
we met by the University Chapel and asked the more mature
Christians to lay hands on us, and pray for us to receive the
baptism of the Holy Spirit. I remember that nothing appeared
to happen to me for a few minutes, but I was told to receive, by
faith. Later I started singing praises but I experienced nothing
physical. Some of my friends had received the baptism of the
Holy Spirit and were speaking in tongues. They were praying
loudly while some of us were singing by faith, afterwards we
returned to our rooms.

The next morning was a Saturday. I washed and dressed, and
went out to the small communal courtyard, where the clothes
lines were, to have some privacy. It was early in the morning,
and very few people were about. As I opened my mouth to
speak quietly, I found I was speaking in tongues! I attempted to
pray again, and had the same experience. I was full of joy, and
attempted it for a third time – forgive me for being a doubting
Thomas – and I was glad that I was on my own for this special
time. I went back to my room to research 'speaking in tongues' in
the Bible, now that I had experienced it for myself. The scripture
that best described my experience was John 7:

> 'In the last day, that great day of the feast, Jesus
> stood and cried, saying, 'If any man thirst, let
> him come unto me, and drink. He that believeth
> in me, as the Scripture hath said, out of his belly
> shall flow rivers of living water.' (But this spoke

He of the Spirit, which they that believe on Him
should receive: for the Holy Ghost was not yet
given; because that Jesus was not yet glorified)'.

John 7:37-39

The move of the Spirit

Things never remained the same, the joy of the Lord was
on my face! My friends and I became hungry and thirsty for His
Spirit. There was a passion for His presence and to share Him
anywhere and everywhere. It was like being in love and unable
to contain one's feelings. In fact, my veterinary colleagues
thought I would not complete my five-year course because, as
newly baptised Christians, we were transformed. We spoke with
authority and, being young, we were full of faith and energy. We
continued to study His word, and to stay grounded in Him and
we challenged any church traditions that contradicted biblical
doctrines. As undergraduates, we had fire in our bellies and
openly defied human traditions, which did us no favours in terms
of building relationships with those around us. I guess we were a
little ahead of ourselves, nonconformists who were going back
to basics. For example, I was told to leave the church meeting
on some occasions for not obeying church rules, such as not
wearing a head covering, wearing make-up, or wearing clothes
with short sleeves. This was to prevent us from corrupting others,
but as young people we were free and we felt convicted that
this behaviour was not sinful. Above all, we wanted to uphold
this new freedom in Christ mentioned in the second chapter of
Colossians as well as the fifth chapter of Galatians!

'Wherefore if ye be dead with Christ from the
rudiments of the world, why, as though living in
the world, are ye subject to ordinances; (touch

not; taste not; handle not; which all are to perish with the using;) after the commandments and doctrines of men?'

Colossians 2:20- 22

'Stand fast therefore in the liberty wherewith Christ hath made us free, and be not entangled again with the yoke of bondage.'

Galatians 5:1

Twelve to fifteen of us were regularly thrown out of meetings for our appearance and not conforming to church traditions, so we started meeting under the tree outside the university chapel on Sunday afternoons. The meetings lasted through to the evening, and the Bible was our only guide. To our amazement, no one dropped off or backslid in spite of being ostracised from the main fellowship. In fact, this worked in our favour. We read in the Psalms that we could lift up holy hands, so we did. We sang, danced, worshipped, lifted our hands and one day, without anyone touching one other, we fell under the power of the Spirit under the trees! The atmosphere of worship was so charged that the presence of the Holy Spirit was surreal. This was a strange new experience. We sang in language we understood, and we also sang in tongues. We prayed in language we understood, and also prayed in tongues. Sometimes, when the Spirit was present to minister, we would be in His presence for hours. As young people we had no other responsibilities, and these meetings mostly took place during weekends, so we were under no time pressure. Those not physically affected used such times to reflect and listen to God; with time, we realised that God loves praise and worship. He also values silence. A few of us received visions and pictures, others manifested gifts of interpretation of tongues, dreams and visions. Some prophesied to individuals or groups. We continually shared scriptures with one another, and listened to teaching to ensure our spirituality was undergirded by the word of God. We also referred back to the Bible continuously to ensure we were not living in error.

> 'And it shall come to pass afterward, that I will pour out my spirit upon all flesh; and your sons and your daughters shall prophesy, your old men shall dream dreams, your young men shall see visions: And also upon the servants and upon the handmaids in those days will I pour out my spirit.'
>
> Joel 2:28-29

This was a new phenomenon. We took turns to lead the group, we studied and shared scriptures and everyone had to be ready to share when called upon. We also read Christian books and, gradually, ministry gifts and leadership traits started manifesting among members of the group. Those with pastoral hearts cared for new Christians, those with the gifts of expositional teaching led cell groups, those with the heart for evangelism went on weekly visitations and those with prophetic gifts shared prophecies as led by the Holy Spirit. We set aside time for ministry where people were healed and delivered. Many were added to our number and, when our group grew too big to meet under the tree, we moved to a large auditorium in the Agricultural Sciences building. About four years after, when I left, there were over three hundred members.

Even though we were committed Christians, none of us dropped out of university. Instead we encouraged each other to be the best for our Saviour. We believed in Paul's model of ministry: serving the Lord and yet working as a tent maker. By divine grace, most of the founding members eventually became Christian leaders in their communities. In spite of doubts and name-calling by other Christians, we stayed true to our calling. Other established campus fellowships doubted our authenticity, but His face shone on us and gave us peace. We articulated our belief in the Messiah, respectfully spoke about the supremacy of Christ, prayed with expectation, distributed material possessions among students in need, paid and managed our tithes, ministered to those without. Many, if not all of us, graduated from the university with flying colours in our professional courses. We exuded confidence in Christ, and became known for exhibiting great faith, challenging the religious status quo yet sharing His grace with anyone and everyone.

A similar phenomenon was taking place 'at the same time' in various universities in Nigeria, such as the University of Lagos, University of Ife, Ekpoma University and Ahmadu Bello University. During term breaks, I had the opportunity to visit these various campuses to preach, lead worship and minister. The zeal of the Lord was moving among Nigerian undergraduates and no establishment could stop it. Scripture was being fulfilled as described in Habakkuk 2:14, 'For the earth will be filled with the knowledge of the glory of the Lord, as the waters cover the sea.' This proves the simplicity of the gospel, if we believe His words then we can manifest spiritual gifts in the twentieth century. For those who believe the era of experiencing these gifts has passed, it is their loss. He is the same yesterday, today and forever!

Service year

After graduating, I was posted to serve with the Nigerian Youth Corp service at Niger State, northern Nigeria in 1987. National youth service was compulsory for all graduates and came with minimal pay. However, it provided 'on-the-job-training', promoted cross-cultural cohesion, supported tolerance and inter-tribal engagement, offered a platform for the development of leadership skills and we all received the same allowance irrespective of profession or education. Youth Corp participants were from all over Nigeria, though a few who studied abroad also joined, because it was a prerequisite for working as a civil servant. Youth service lasted for one year, and people could be posted to either urban or rural areas. Prior to stationing, everyone posted to Niger state camped together for a month at Bida Polytechnic during the summer vacation. There could be as many as 1,000 participants, mostly graduates from Nigerian higher education institutions.

As in any community, shared interests bring groups together, and we were living together as young professionals on site. We had military personnel on site to administer the programme, like army cadets, instilling order and discipline for thirty days before being placed on an assignment relevant to each person's qualifications. For many, this was their first taste of freedom. We had language classes together, in my case we studied Hausa. We ate together three times a day in the dining hall. We wore khaki uniforms during the day, and were assigned to different duties on site. Medics ran the sick-bay, and agriculturists led the farm duties on the large farmlands, cultivated and maintained by us, called 'Corpers'. For many city people, this was their first introduction to farming, in temperatures as high as 42°C! My friend was the librarian, so I assisted her in the library because my skills set as a vet were not required on site. As this was a community of largely unsupervised young professionals, potential leaders developed in various circles. We had exercises early in the morning and came together for a short time in the evening. There was a tuck shop managed by students too, and we all received an allowance, though we were fed and clothed by the government. It was fun, and a great way of networking and making friends from all over the country. In spite of the busy schedule, everyone gravitated to their groups of interest because our evenings were free. We had those partying each day, those discussing politics, guys seeking ladies for short- or long-term friendships, and the intellectual types. Just like life at university. Within this community were Christians wishing to make their voice heard and have a positive impact.

On the first day of arrival, mature Christians living in Bida town and those who served in the previous year would visit the campus to inform us about the active interdenominational Christian fellowship on site. There was a meeting every evening and during the day we had work assigned to us, visiting civic centres, traditional leaders and government dignitaries. Basically, we chose our friends, our lifestyles and decided upon our futures. One of the reasons for the early intervention of Christians was the fear of losing members to other groups. Since we were in camp for only one month, Christian leaders were conscious and protective of vulnerable young Christians being enticed away from the Christian faith. Once identified as a Christian, we were protected from outsiders and I imagine we were also studied by Christian brothers seeking potential friends or future life partners. This was a safe place to get to know one another before being posted to who knows where!

The Christian Fellowship was a launching ground for us. During the week we focused on evangelism and introduced friends to Jesus. At weekends we planned crusades, participated at Christian conferences or visited nearby churches. Our gifts and callings came in useful and I quickly slotted into the praying ministry, though I was comfortable preaching and teaching scriptures as well. Prayers before services offered support and assistance to the new converts. There were those with social, spiritual and emotional challenges. At our fellowship there were healings, prophesies, words of wisdom, words of knowledge, we spoke in tongues and interpreted tongues. There were also requests for deliverance, particularly for those who had dabbled in the occult or exposed themselves consciously or unconsciously to wrong spirits. The most common complaints were those with persistent bad dreams.

The camp was a melting point of cultures, with many faiths, practices and interests. The Christian fellowship was like the counselling and support centre, because we operated every evening and confidentiality was guaranteed. My university campus experience came in handy, and I was a very active Christian. We were invited to minister at the *Full Gospel Business Men & Women's Fellowship* as well as popular independent ministries in Bida town. We shared, prayed, debated and ministered together. We became one big family, and supported each other after we were sent to new stations, particularly those posted to rural dwellings far from the capital. Our friendships lasted long beyond our service years, and many later became church leaders in their own right. I met my husband during my service year and settled in Minna, capital of Niger State. It was there that we had our two children.

'Now there are diversities of gifts, but the same Spirit. And there are differences of administrations, but the same Lord. And there are diversities of operations, but it is the same God which worketh all in all. But the manifestation of the Spirit is given to every man to profit withal. For to one is given by the Spirit the word of wisdom; to another the word of knowledge by the same Spirit; to another faith by the same Spirit; to another the gifts of healing by the same Spirit; to another the working of miracles; to another prophecy; to another discerning of spirits; to another divers kinds of tongues; to another the interpretation of tongues. But all these worketh that one and the selfsame Spirit, dividing to every man severally as He will. For as the body is one, and hath many members, and all the members of that one body, being many, are one body: so also is Christ.'

1 Corinthians 12:4-12

Living by faith

After Youth Corp service and my marriage, even though I had a secular and well-paid job, I was still very passionate about extending His work and my husband was supportive of this. We joined a newly- founded independent ministry at Minna and, even though we were only seven members when we joined, three years later, membership exceeded five hundred. We had no support from external partners; we believed in Him for all the resources we required, and the church building was constructed after we contributed to purchase the land. Ade was ordained as an Elder and I was appointed a Deaconess. I led the Women's Ministry and the prayer group. About four years after we were married, we had two children. Then, after I completed my training, I enrolled with the Child Evangelism Ministry and became a Sunday school teacher. In addition to that, I conducted Bible kids club at home, which hosted up to fifty kids from the neighbourhood every week.

Training with Child Evangelism Ministry was prompted by Him. I was seeking His face, and offering our service as a missionary family willing to serve anywhere people were reluctant to go, including remote villages. I believe the response I heard from the Holy Spirit was for us to raise our children to fear Him. That was how we became involved in Children's ministry, and of course this helped in raising our own children – Gboyega and Funke. I was glad we had a daughter and, considering our missionary aspirations, two children were sufficient. He was very good to us!

We were well settled in Minna; I worked in Veterinary Public

Health and was responsible for meat and milk hygiene, in addition to disease reporting and control for farm animals. Ade worked with the UNDP (United Nations Development Programme), and both children attended good nursery schools.

The call

The idea was to buy few cows and employ someone to rear them alongside the nomadic Fulani tribe in the locality. Then, during church fundraising for the land purchase, I felt the Lord telling us to sell it and sow the money as a seed. It was a prize heifer. Ade agreed to sell the heifer and we gave the proceeds to the church as a sacrifice of thanksgiving to God. Not long afterwards, sometime in November 1994, we were called to serve abroad, in Belfast, Northern Ireland. Never in my wildest dreams did I expect this! I thought we would be used in a rural African village. So I asked the Lord why He was sending an African woman with two children? How would I have the opportunity to minister and serve, since I knew no one in Belfast? I knew that the call to Belfast did not come from me, because I knew no one there, but I believe the Lord responded by saying, 'when I call you; I shall make a way, and create opportunities for you', and of course He did!

> 'I have been young, and now am old; yet have I not seen the righteous forsaken, nor his seed begging bread.'
>
> Psalm 37:25-30

I can testify of how wonderful and thrilling it is to serve God, He is reliable and always right on time even though many times we might have to live on the edge! Be assured, that although our faith is stretched, we will learn how to hear and obey our loving Father.

Questions to ponder

❖ Have you ever earnestly desired a spiritual gift?
❖ How has it transformed you?
❖ What is your relationship with the Holy Spirit?

God is good
He has done me well
O my soul
Rise up and
Praise the Lord
      Afro-Caribbean fellowship,
         Edinburgh 1993-94

Mission Call

'Now unto Him that is able to do exceeding abundantly above all that we ask or think, according to the power that worketh in us, Unto him be glory in the church by Christ Jesus throughout all ages, Jesus world without end. Amen.'

Ephesians 3: 20 – 21

Lift off

Now that we knew we were leaving, we shared our vision with friends and family. We had to decide what to leave behind and what to take with us, and we gave away household items. We agreed that we would depart during my annual leave towards the end of 1995, so I resigned from my job.

The children said their goodbyes at school and we were sent off by faith by our community at the Living Faith Church, Minna in Nigeria. Then we all travelled to Lagos. Ade stayed behind to tie up loose ends in Minna before relocating to his organisation's headquarters at Abuja, Nigeria. I was departing for the UK with the children, hoping against hope that Ade would join us as soon as possible after I had obtained appropriate accommodation, a good job and sufficient funds in our bank account. We purchased our flight tickets, said farewell to friends and family, and prayed for favour. Then we embarked on our journey to the UK via Bulgaria, which made the journey just about affordable.

Since we travelled in November 1995 it was already very cold in Europe, especially at Sophia airport. My daughter Funke slid on black ice and fell, while walking to the airport terminal after disembarking from the plane. This was her first experience of walking on icy ground. She was only four years old, and she clung to me from then onwards.

Next, we took a flight to Heathrow airport, and found that the airport workers there were on strike. The queues were so long, and I was coping with the tiring journey, two young children and a large amount of luggage. There was no one to meet us at the airport. My sister was living in London, pursuing her postgraduate certificate in Education. She had a lot on her plate, and I did not want to burden her with my issues. I also did not want people to divert or distract me from God's call with opinions and suggestions. As the Lord would have it, one of the British Airways ground crew was very kind and offered help when she noticed that I had luggage for three, plus young children.

We had no tickets for our onward trip to Belfast, so I had to pay double the price. This was a big dent in our initial maintenance budget for settling in Belfast. I just had to live by faith knowing that God, who had called us, was faithful.

We arrived at Belfast International airport and I called a friend's cousin living in Bangor whose phone number I was given. The person apologised for being unable to help, and hung up the phone. Considering the obvious differences between the Nigerian and UK cultures, I do understand now how daunting it must have been. What I needed most was some guidance and information about places to stay in Belfast. I eventually got our baggage on a trolley.

The children were tired from two days' travel in the cold; they were also hungry and ready for bed. At the airport, using a payphone, I phoned around to find a guest house in Belfast during the busy Belfast festival season. I found decent bed and breakfast on Eglantine Street, near Queen's University, and we took a taxi. The room was very cold because the landlady had not been expecting us, but the children had hot chocolate with biscuits for their evening tea and I got them tucked into bed after a short prayer. They fell asleep with not a care in the world.

On my knees

After feeding the children, I also had a hot drink and a biscuit, which was all I could afford. Then I knelt down by my bed and thanked God for journey mercies, and for providing for us all the way. I told the Lord that I had reached my destination, and was waiting for His instructions. Here I am Lord, use me!

As I reflected, I recalled that John the Baptist started his ministry at age thirty, Christ started his at age thirty, and David started reigning as king at age thirty. So that had to be a significant number in ministry. Interestingly, I was thirty years of age when I arrived at this country, waiting obediently for God's instruction.

After all our travel expenses I checked my purse and realised that I had just enough money to pay for one more night's accommodation. Without getting anxious, I asked for divine guidance and intervention because we read in Psalm 37:23 that 'The steps of a good man are ordered by the Lord'. All I needed was a good sleep, so that I could figure out what the next step was!

I woke early and refreshed the next morning, dressed the children, and we had a lovely breakfast. I thought that was probably the last full meal I could afford. Once more, the Lord intervened. I asked for a housing advice office close to the Bed & Breakfast, and was directed to Belfast City Centre Housing Executive headquarters. We went there and, by His grace, we were given a room at the Salvation Army hostel in north Belfast. It was a miracle! The Salvation Army officers were very kind and I was very grateful that it was managed by Christians. Then I asked about Primary Schools close by. There were a few, and I settled on Cavehill Primary School which was about thirty to forty minutes' walk from Glen Alva Hostel. This was another miracle because we arrived during term time, so finding school places just before Christmas was not easy. Moreover, I wanted them both to go to the same primary school, and the Lord made a way for us. After sorting out schools and accommodation, I called my sister and told her we were in Belfast. All we had to consider were school uniforms, finding warm clothing, and getting to know our new neighbourhood. The Lord had done it again, and I was so thankful and joyful.

Sunday worship

Sunday came, and I was looking forward to going to church. But which church? I woke the children early, we dressed, ate and were ready. I asked for the nearest Elim Pentecostal Church, which was on Alexander Park, and we went there by taxi because it was cold and we did not know our way around. In agreement with Psalm 122:1, 'I was glad when they said unto me, 'Let us go into the house of the Lord". I knew I would get support and guidance about what to do next. I needed to thank Him, meet with His people and understand His plan for us in Belfast. It was a brilliant service and the people were very nice. We were the only Africans and the first to ever worship there, so there were lots of questions. I became involved with church activities right away, and started seeking work so that my husband could join us. I knew would not reach my final destination, until I found where He wanted me to serve.

Success comes from managed think

The Lord blessed us with friends and well-wishers who supported us in that community. Now I understand the gravity of moving to a new country with young children, and I try to come alongside such families when I encounter them, to provide practical and spiritual help. I remember Bishop Oyedepo once said, 'when you act out your belief – that is faith!'. As we settled into our routine at the hostel, I got up at five o'clock each day, as if I was already working. I had my quiet time and prepared the children for school. Since we were living in a hostel it was important to get in to the bathroom early, or you would have to wait for everyone else to use the bathroom and toilet facilities before you could have access. Bathrooms were shared and we had to tell the cook what our family wanted for breakfast After eating, we all walked to school because the bus arrive I times were too erratic. We walked through the water works and admired the swans swimming in the man-made ponds on the site. On arrival, I handed them over to their class teachers or classroom assistants, because we often arrived early. I would then take the bus to the Queen's University library to hunt for jobs using the newspapers and publications there, as well as to read about the new country and culture. I would then have to leave in plenty of time to collect the children from school, and we would walk back home.

Job hunting

Bob was the Centre supervisor. He was a lovely committed Christian and a member of the Salvation Army. He advised me to buy the Belfast Telegraph for job adverts. I remember the first time I bought the paper and was amazed at the number of jobs advertised. I was very excited, though Bob cautioned me that gaining employment in Northern Ireland was not an easy feat. I really did not understand what he meant, but sometimes ignorance is bliss. I regularly completed and submitted application forms and received quite a few interviews even though I was told work was difficult to come by. This meant handling a new challenge; I needed a childminder because I hardly knew anyone. The school would only release the children to me or a registered childminder. So I contacted a registered childminder from the list provided, to help mind Gboyega and Funke whilst I went for an interview. I did not know that to apply for a job I needed a reference from friends, this made it even more difficult. After my interview, when I returned to collect my children, the childminder was smoking and swearing in front of them; I was horrified.

I needed a job to enable my husband to join us, and so that we did not become a burden on the state. Moreover I knew God did not call me to leave a well-paid professional job in Nigeria to be claiming benefits in Northern Ireland. I renegotiated with Him after my experience with the childminder. I was no longer looking for well-paid jobs but a good job that would permit me to raise my kids in a godly fashion. In addition to that, I wanted an affordable accommodation that would meet the needs of my family. Within months, He did it! I was given a tied accommodation with my job, so that I could mind the children when they were off school, because my office was below our three-bedroomed maisonette. Though it was not a highly paid job, it was a perfect job. We moved from north Belfast to just off the Lisburn Road area, near south Belfast. I was living on site so I could care for the children over the long summer holidays, or when the kids were ill, without needing a childminder. What a great help it was, not having to pay for childcare. I cannot thank Him enough for His kindness in answering my prayers.

Not only that, with my meagre salary I could not afford to pay for tutors. Instead I prepared the children for their eleven plus examinations in addition to other personal development. In addition, the children had their usual extracurricular activities such as swimming and music lessons after school. They had great fun at home, at the park and we all went to church together regularly. The icing on the cake was that my work place was close to Queen's University, enabling me to take professional management courses paid for by my employer. Our Father is indeed wonderful. I cannot thank Him enough for His goodness and mercies on us as a family. He does answer prayers!

New ministry

When we moved near the Lisburn Road in south Belfast, we had to change church. We left Alexandra Road Elim, where we had been so well supported by Christians as we settled in our new home. We then sampled various churches close by, including Brethren, Salvation Army, and Belfast City Mission. One of my work colleagues, who knew that I was passionate about seeking a home church, took me to her childhood church – the Ulster Temple, Elim Pentecostal. The moment I stepped inside the church, it was as if a star descended upon the building, and I knew this was where He was sending me! This was why I had left Minna for Belfast! I explained earlier how the Pastor of the Elim Church had been praying for an intercessor and, when we eventually met, he asked what my interest was. I told him that I had several interests, but the ministry I most wished to engage in was intercessory prayer. Thereafter, I became an active church member and, among other things, led the prayer school, which conducted monthly night vigils, participated in Saturday early morning prayers and breakfast meetings. On Sundays I led the 'one hour prayer time' before service, where scriptural prayers became the norm and we experienced beautiful times during pre-service worship. By the time the main service was in full swing, ministry was easy, and ran alongside wonderful bible expositions. I had a wonderful eleven years at Ulster Temple, and it was great to witness the church going from strength to strength.

In my last few years at Ulster Temple, I became the Mission Secretary and liaised with mission partners. In collaboration with church members and other churches, we organised short-term group mission visits and two long-term mission placements. I conducted regular prayers for mission on the last Sunday evening of each month, distributed newsletters among supporters, updated stakeholders and arranged fundraising activities with various church members. The Lord proved Himself again and again and I am forever indebted to Him. It is true that self-talk determines where you arrive in life.

Questions to ponder

- ❖ Have you experienced the need for immediate obedience?
- ❖ How did you deal with it?
- ❖ Are you considering a mission call upon your life?

Izmir - Turkey

CHAPTER 12

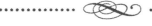

Stormy Times

'These things I have spoken unto you, that in me ye might have peace. In the world ye shall have tribulation: but be of good cheer; I have overcome the world.'

John 16:33

Family reunion

The Lord provided us with good accommodation, a great job and the children were settled at Forge Integrated Primary School in Belfast. We met the Home Office prerequisites for Ade to leave his top job with UNDP in Nigeria. Two years later he was able to join us and we were overjoyed as a family. We had great plans, we attended church together, and soon he was to start work.

But it was not as easy as we had expected. It was difficult for Ade to achieve a similar status of work. Perhaps it was easier for me to blend, having spent longer in the UK. Also, I was much younger and more able to adapt, whereas Ade was older than me, and unused to the UK work culture. To compound issues, Ade is a Prince; his father was the Olojudo of Iddo Ekiti, a first class Yoruba king and direct descendant of Oduduwa, the Father of all Yorubas. His father was a close ally of Chief Awolowo, the first Premier of the Western Region after Nigerian independence. His father was one of the dignitaries that hosted the Queen of England during her visit to Nigeria prior to independence in 1956. Though he was of a royal line and a very intelligent man, he struggled with the persistent challenges of settling in this new culture. He was eventually given various short-term contracts here and there. By this time, the children were ready for grammar schools in Belfast and that was when I lost my mum to breast cancer. With so many ongoing changes, it was time for me to move on; new job, new house, new neighbourhood.

Move to the village

I can still recall the face of my pastor, Pastor Hamilton, when I told him we were moving to the Village by the Donegal Road in south Belfast. He was stunned. He asked if that was my only option, and I responded that it was. I knew that to progress in life, we had to take risks (Hybels, 2011). The children were approaching teenage years and we needed more funds for their grammar schools. I was very thankful that they had both performed well in their 'eleven plus' school entrance examinations and proceeded to top Belfast schools. Gboyega went to the all-boys Royal Belfast Institution and Funke went to Victoria College, the female counterpart. Gboyega was an ardent Rugby player and Funke was involved in the debating society. As I prayed over the need for more income, God was my only resort, and He was very faithful. I found work at Queen's University but that meant leaving our cosy three-bedroomed maisonette near the Lisburn Road. Since the salary was not much, we were only just able to scrape together the funds to pay for a house deposit. Thankfully, we had the opportunity to buy a boarded-up Housing Executive (local authority) property in the village, which was all that we could afford!

In perfect timing, we moved in the summer, just before Funke started grammar school. However, this neighbourhood was much further away from the university, and the children had no friends in the community. The area was known for its Loyalist paramilitary activities. Both children were now in grammar schools quite a distance from home, and we were also much further removed from our church; Ulster Temple, Elim Pentecostal on Ravenhill Road.

Not long after we moved to the village, there were spates of racist attacks against Africans, but the Lord preserved us. Some Africans in the neighbourhood were verbally attacked and a few had petrol bombs thrown into their homes. We had very good immediate neighbour. Barbara, Angela and Nat, members of our church in the Village, also supported us. We had our windows broken a few times and dung thrown into the back of the house but He protected us. A number of broadcast media channels interviewed me for television and radio after these incidents; however, I was at peace. The Bible confirms that mission is not always easy; Jesus and his disciples had their own share of hardships. Early missionaries who travelled globally sharing the gospel encountered hardships. My children coped well, but things came to a head when family friends were being stoned in their vehicles when visiting us.

All these events had an adverse effect on Ade. Despite being in the UK for a few years, he was still unsettled, and not coping well. To avoid a downward spiral of his well-being, we agreed it was better that he move to his brother's place in London for a while. The whole family could not move with him for many reasons, therefore we needed a breakthrough - He did it again.

Light at the end of the tunnel

The children excelled in school, in spite of the challenging situation at home. I was well supported at work and at church and, as a family, we were very positive. Every morning and evening, I was able to prayer walk in my neighbourhood. I was not afraid at all, instead I was grateful for His protection and provision. These experiences made me more sensitive to visitors, foreigners and the homeless in our community. I prayed better for the homeless and those experiencing hardship. We were no different from the locals experiencing sectarianism, and we all needed His healing and love. After two years at my work place in the university, I had the opportunity to move to a higher position at work, and move out of the village. Close to the Belfast Bible School at Dunmurry, this new home was very different from our property in the village. It was so peaceful, like heaven on earth! To further marvel at His grace, a Belfast solicitor took up my case with the government and forced the Housing Executive to buy the last house back from me. This freed up mortgage payments for the new property, which was such a blessing. Our new house was very accessible to public transport, which helped me when I was unable to pick up the children from after-school activities.

Unexpected change

The new home was great in terms of location and comfort, my young adults were progressing well, and Ade was temporarily in London before crossing over to Bristol. Bob Gass the author of 'Word for Today', said that 'career is what you are paid for; calling is what you are made for'. I was fulfilled in my ministry and knew that when the Spirit blew and the cloud lifted, that it would be time to move, but I must confess that I did not see it coming.

My son had just completed his GCSEs and my daughter was preparing for hers. Nevertheless, my workplace at the university was undergoing major restructuring. Initially I was unconcerned, because I knew I was doing a great job; my work was necessary and important. I believed that as a Christian, the Lord would protect me, but I was about to be flabbergasted. We were all advised to reapply for our jobs, and the timing could not have been worse. I submitted my application, as the others did, and was awaiting the result. All of a sudden, I felt the Holy Spirit warn me to look out for another job. I would forever be grateful for that word of wisdom! Three months later we were offered voluntary redundancy and I was the only one to take up the offer. Two months after the Holy Spirit alerted me, I started a job with the Church Mission Society (CMS) in London! All the jobs in Belfast seemed to have dried up for me. It was just before the financial crisis in 2007, the property market was booming, and there were high expectations of improved living standards.

My son did well in his GCSE exams and decided to remain at school for 'A' levels. It was too late to move my daughter to England. If I did not take up the job, how would we meet our financial needs? All we could do was trust in God, and once again I was on my knees.

The severance package helped with my accommodation in London and, shortly afterwards, CMS moved from London to Oxford. Oxford property prices were as expensive as they were in London; however God did it again

I had to fly to Belfast each month to support the children, and attend school events and information evenings. I also had to accompany them to university interviews, pay the bills and stock up the pantry with food supplies, leaving the house in good condition for the next few weeks. I could not have done it without God's kindness, nor without the children being responsible and studious. Both had part-time jobs, both were prefects and had to prepare for important examinations. Gboyega was part of his school rugby team, which won the Belfast rugby tournament in 2007. Funke undertook volunteer work places to build up her medical school entry portfolio. Through it all, they still attended church services. Funke was a Sunday school teacher and helped with the younger children. Even though Gboyega was an ardent rugby player, by God's grace he found time to attend church. This was the doing of the Lord and marvelous in our eyes. It is true that often we thrive in life, through times of adversity.

God is faithful

Philip Baker writes that a focussed life is a simple and motivated one. God is far more interested in our being, than our doing. Even though the cost of accommodation was rising, I believed Him for another miracle. I agree with Baker when he says wealth is not linked to human resource but human creativity. Somehow I believed I could have a small place of my own, rather than wasting money on rent. An Oxford estate agent told me about a lovely new flat in Witney, about twenty miles from Oxford. I had never been there before, but took on the challenge. Baker says in his book *let your 'why nots' exceed your 'what ifs'*. I just had faith that He would grant me a creative mental attitude, and that I would succeed in life. It happened! In truth, thinking regulates action as Joseph Murphy states in his book, *The Power of Your Unconscious Mind*. Eventually He provided me with a flat in a miraculous way, so that I did not have to beg, borrow or steal in spite of everything else that was going on at the time. I was able to have my own space, as well as travelling to Belfast by air every month to check on the children.

I remember when direct flights to Belfast were stopped by one of the budget airlines. I had to travel to Dublin, in the Republic of Ireland, and travel by road for about two hours to Belfast. Since I had to depend on public transport, my regular travel times were extended, and I needed to be back in the office by Monday morning. throughout, my Father was faithful. How I coped financially and otherwise, only He knew. He is truly awesome, it was another miracle.

A near-miss accident

> 'When thou passest through the waters, I will be with thee; and through the rivers, they shall not overflow thee: when thou walkest through the fire, thou shalt not be burned; neither shall the flame kindle upon thee.'
>
> Isaiah 43:2

Sometimes I felt overwhelmed, but He always saw me through. I was blessed with very good health, and consistently surrounded with favour. Since moving to England in 2007, I had travelled to visit Ade in Bristol weekly for more than five years until I encountered a near-miss accident. On the way home on the M4 motorway, between Witney and Bristol, I lost control of my vehicle and it rotated by about three hundred degrees, stopping against the direction of travel of the vehicles on the motorway. I placed my head on the steering wheel and asked if it was time to come home? I was very calm and called out His name. My vehicle was in the middle of the motorway, facing in the wrong direction, on a busy Sunday evening. I lifted my head, and all the vehicles stopped a few yards in front of my car. There was no accident, and once again I praised Him! I restarted my vehicle and drove to the hard shoulder, where I calmed down, said my prayers and set off slowly back to Witney in Oxfordshire, thanking the Lord.

It was very surprising that there was no damage to the vehicle, and that I was able to return home without roadside assistance. I was driving at motorway speed, and yet none of the vehicles around me were involved in an accident. I shared the testimony at my church the following day, and the congregation members thanked the Lord with me! I cannot tell all that the Lord has done for me.

However, I can definitely say that serving Him is exciting and rewarding. My life has been full of twists and turns; nonetheless it is always best to be at the centre of His will. Bill Hybels put it very well when he said, 'the gentle shall outlast the strong, the obscure outlasts the obvious!' I am only alive by His grace.

Questions to ponder

- ❖ How did God see you through your storms?
- ❖ Looking back, what have you learnt?
- ❖ Did you take time to share His faithfulness?

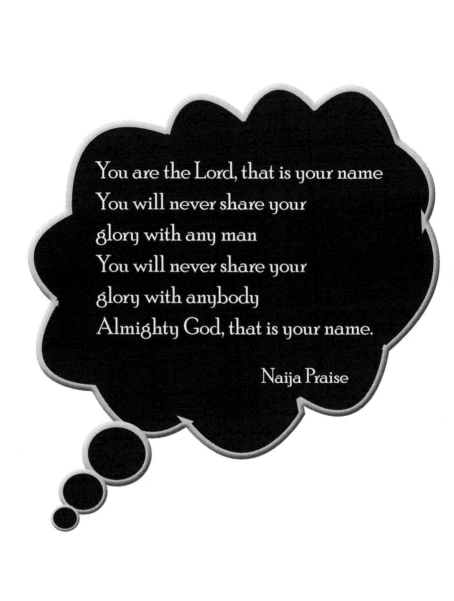

You are the Lord, that is your name
You will never share your
glory with any man
You will never share your
glory with anybody
Almighty God, that is your name.

Naija Praise

CHAPTER 13

How great is our God?

'Although the fig tree shall not blossom, neither shall fruit be in the vines; the labour of the olive shall fail, and the fields shall yield no meat; the flock shall be cut off from the fold, and there shall be no herd in the stalls: yet I will rejoice in the Lord, I will rejoice in the God of my salvation. The Lord God is my strength, and he will make my feet like hinds' feet, and he will make me to walk upon mine high places.'

Habakkuk 3:17-19

Mum's testimony

You may be wondering how I related with my mum after the earlier encounter. I am glad to say that we had a wonderful relationship. She was very concerned about my whereabouts after I left home, and was relieved to know that I had stayed safely at school all that while.

The year I graduated, I went for youth service and I was married to Ade before my service year ended. Mum came to live with us briefly in Minna, Niger state, to help with childminding when I had my second child, a daughter. My mum was amazing, very easy and laid back. She eventually gave her life to Christ and became a Methodist, attending the same church where my father's dad had served as an elder during his lifetime: the Methodist Church Oshodi, in Lagos. She was a committed and active church member, and a born again Christian. I was very proud of her. She was a very kind and driven woman. After her separation from my dad, she had to provide for herself, since most of us were then graduates and living away from home. Maintenance payments are not easy to come by in sub-Saharan Africa. When separated, you just get on with life. I guess her life experience made me more determined to succeed in life, and trust Him totally.

Handling disappointments

Even Christians encounter disappointments. On the 5 July 2001, I lost my mum to breast cancer at the age of sixty-five. She was a very industrious and compassionate woman, and my mentor. She threw away of the 'unpleasant charm' that I mentioned previously, and made her home a transit lodge for her children's friends in need of accommodation. When any of our friends found themselves stranded in Lagos, we directed them to mum. There were no mobile phones in those days, so our friends only had to call and mention their children's names and their circumstances, and they could be accommodated temporarily.

Every time we visited the family house, there were different temporary residents there. They were mostly undergraduates and young professionals seeking residence in Lagos, Nigeria. This meant that mum was hardly ever alone in the house. Her faith in Christ grew stronger until she passed away. The last time I was with her, she asked me to pray with her. By then the breast cancer had spread throughout her internal organs and I knew it was the last time I would see her alive. A few weeks after our encounter, she told my immediate junior brother that she was tired, and ready to go to heaven after his wedding. She managed to fulfil her wish of attending his wedding, and she passed away a few weeks after.

My greatest hope is that I will see her again in heaven! I was asked at the time if I was upset because God did not heal her? Some asked if I still believed in divine healing. Of course I did! God is sovereign, and I do not know His plans. I cannot limit His abilities to my limited life experience.

> 'The secret things belong unto the Lord our God: but those things which are revealed belong unto us and to our children forever, that we may do all the words of this law.'
>
> (Deuteronomy 29:29)

Handling persistent concerns

I am often asked how to know when we should stop praying, even though a prayer request seems to remain unanswered? I do not have a ready-made answer, except to say that He is sovereign, and He chooses how to respond in each circumstance. Nevertheless, I can list few different prayer styles I have adopted from the Bible. There are numerous prayer styles, but I have limited myself to a few, listed below:

1. Hannah's approach – 1 Samuel 1:12-18

> 'And Eli said unto her, 'How long wilt thou be drunken?' Put away thy wine from thee'. And Hannah answered and said, 'No, my lord, I am a woman of a sorrowful spirit: I have drunk neither wine nor strong drink, but have poured out my soul before the Lord. Count not thine handmaid for a daughter of Belial: for out of the abundance of my complaint and grief have I spoke hitherto.' Then Eli answered and said,' 'Go in peace': and the God of Israel grant thee thy petition that thou hast asked of Him'. And she said, 'Let thine handmaid find grace in thy sight'. 'So the woman went her way, and did eat, and her countenance was no more sad'.'
>
> 1 Samuel 1:12-18

Hannah was concerned about not having a child, and prayed year-in and year-out. However, on this occasion, she was embittered and mumbled in her heart. Eli thought she was drunk, though he changed his mind after speaking with her, and supported Hannah's prayer request. Hannah's countenance changed immediately after Eli had prayed for her (not just when she arrived home, or discovered she was pregnant). This tells me that sometimes we can respond in faith to a word of assurance from the Lord or from one of His servants.

2. David's approach – 2 Samuel 12:13-20

> 'And David said unto Nathan, 'I have sinned against the Lord.' And Nathan said unto David, 'The Lord also hath put away thy sin; thou shalt not die'. Howbeit, because by this deed thou

hast given great occasion to the enemies of the Lord to blaspheme, the child also that is born unto thee shall surely die.' And Nathan departed unto his house. And the Lord struck the child that Uriah's wife bore to David, and it was very sick. David therefore besought God for the child; and David fasted, and went in, and lay all night upon the earth. And the elders of his house arose, and went to him, to raise him up from the earth: but he would not, neither did he eat bread with them. And it came to pass on the seventh day that the child died. And the servants of David feared to tell him that the child was d ad: for they said, Behold, while the child was yet alive, we spoke unto him, and he would not harken unto our voice: how will he then vex himself, if we tell him that the child is dead? But when David saw that his servants whispered, David perceived that the child was dead: therefore David said unto his servants, 'Is the child dead?' And they said, 'He is dead.' Then David arose from the earth, and washed, and anointed himself, and changed his apparel, and came into the house of the Lord and worshipped: then he went to his own house; and when he required, they set bread before him, and he ate.'

2 Samuel 12:13-20

Nathan, a prophet of God, told David that his son would die as punishment for committing adultery with Bathsheba. David did all he could to change God's mind, and save the innocent child. In the end, the child died. How did David respond? He got up, ate and went to the temple to worship. Sometimes we do our best and, if the outcome is discouraging, we cry, grieve, acknowledge Him as supreme and move on. There is no need for a long period of regret or bitterness.

3. Hezekiah's approach – 2 Kings 20:1-7

> 'In those days was Hezekiah sick unto death. And the prophet Isaiah the son of Amoz came to him, and said unto him, 'Thus saith the Lord, set thine house in order; for thou shalt die, and not live.' Then he turned his face to the wall, and prayed unto the Lord, saying, 'I beseech thee, O Lord, remember now how I have walked before thee in truth and with a perfect heart, and have done that which is good in thy sight.' And Hezekiah wept sore. And it came to pass, afore Isaiah was gone out into the middle court, that the word of the Lord came to him, saying, 'Turn again, and tell Hezekiah the captain of my people, Thus saith the Lord, the God of David thy father, I have heard thy prayer, I have seen thy tears: behold, I will heal thee: on the third day thou shalt go up unto the house of the Lord. And I will add unto thy days fifteen years; and I will deliver thee and this city out of the hand of the king of Assyria; and I will defend this city for mine own sake, and for my servant David's sake.' And Isaiah said, 'Take a lump of figs'. And they took and laid it on the boil, and he recovered.'
>
> 2 Kings 20:1-7

Hezekiah was told by Isaiah to prepare for his death, and he wept and cried to Him pleading his case. God changed His mind, and granted him an extra fifteen years. Hezekiah was persistent in prayer and did not accept the first verdict – to die very soon. He pleaded his case, and Jehovah yielded. This was a great outcome, although some people wonder if the added fifteen years were helpful to him and Israel! This shows that God may change His mind, if we can objectively present our petitions to Him

4. The persistent widow's approach: Luke 18:2-8

> 'Saying, there was in a city a judge, which feared not God, neither regarded man: And there was a widow in that city; and she came unto him, saying, 'Avenge me of mine adversary'. And he would not for a while: but afterward he said within himself, though I fear not God, nor regard man; Yet because this widow troubleth me, I will avenge her, lest by her continual coming she weary me. And the Lord said, 'Hear what the unjust judge saith. And shall not God avenge his own elect, which cry day and night unto him, though he bear long with them? I tell you that he will avenge them speedily. Nevertheless when the Son of man cometh, shall he find faith on the earth?' '
>
> Luke 18:2-8

The persistent widow had no alternative except to give up, but she did not. The judge was worn out, and eventually granted her wish. So, when do you stop praying over your requests? My suggestion is to continue praying until you sense a blessed assurance within. Then you can shift from 'petition mode' to 'thanksgiving mode'. This supports expectation of divine interventions, since the Lord will hear your cry like He did Hannah, Hezekiah and the persistent widow. Keep on believing. Keep on praising. Keep on expecting your faith to move mountains. If your request is not granted, would He still be your God, or would you give up? In my opinion, Habakkuk 3:18-19 said it best.

Yet I will rejoice in the Lord, I will rejoice in the God of my salvation. The Lord God is my strength, and he will make my feet like hinds' feet, and he will make me to walk upon mine high places.

Know who you are in Christ

As you read this book, I pray that you will continue to discover who you are in Christ, so that you can enjoy Him and enjoy life in the love of God.

> 'For I am persuaded, that neither death, nor life, nor angels, nor principalities, nor powers, nor things present, nor things to come, nor height, nor depth, nor any other creature, shall be able to separate us from the love of God, which is in Christ Jesus our Lord.'
>
> Romans 8:38-39

Irrespective of what you do or who you are, our greatest asset in life is being connected to God. Some boast of their links with royalty, others with famous personalities. However, we put our trust in the name of the Lord! Do not let your age, gender, race, occupation, society, friends, or other life challenges discourage you or tell you otherwise. It is true that 'who you know' matters, and you know the Almighty! As written in Psalm 20: 7-8

'Some trust in chariots, and some in horses: but we will remember the name of the Lord our God. They are brought down and fallen: but we are risen, and stand upright.'

Therefore, we need to keep our angels busy fighting our causes on our behalf. I call my two angels assigned to follow me daily for the rest of my life 'GOODNESS' and 'MERCY' (I have no theological basis for the choice of names; however, they get the job done). Angels are eager to ensure our case files are presented before the Almighty and endorsed by Jesus, our High Priest. However, our words and faith either activate or deactivate them. What's more, we have the mind of Christ, as outlined in 1 Corinthians 2:16. Having the mind of Christ is one of our best assets. What does it mean? To me, it means I can think and reason like Christ.

One of my shortcomings is my not knowing when to talk or to be silent. I admire the ability the Messiah had to think on His feet, be gentle with the vulnerable but firm with the Pharisees. It would be great to be a wonderful communicator like Christ, asking thought-provoking and challenging questions as and when required. Jesus was humble, able to relate to the marginalised, and be compassionate with the weak, yet radical enough to challenge the customs of His day.

To have the mind of Christ offers the ability to work smartly, be a pioneer and align ourselves to His will. I regularly have to pray for wisdom and favour to function well in all capacities. Having His mind should spur creativity and confidence in us so as to distinguish us for greatness. He has given us all things that pertain to life and godliness.

> 'According as his divine power hath given unto us all things that pertain unto life and godliness, through the knowledge of Him that hath called us to glory and virtue:'
>
> 2 Peter 1:3

Having the mind of Christ helps us understand and appreciate what is important to Him – sharing His love, showing compassion, pursuing peace and seeking justice. As disciples of Christ, we should truly reflect His nature as we relate with humanity and with Him. May we understand the times and seasons of His timetable as He shares His secrets with us. May we also exude His anointing, because Jesus is the same yesterday, today and forever

Enjoy God, enjoy life

Many still do not know my Lord, and many have not encountered Him due to fear or ignorance. As we worship and honour Him, He fills our heart with joy and godly pleasures.

> 'Thou wilt shew me the path of life: in thy presence is fullness of joy; at thy right hand there are pleasures for evermore.'
>
> Psalm 16:11

Christianity is exciting and creative. God was the first landscape architect, and He handed His creation over to Adam and Eve to care for it. He did not burden them only with responsibilities but ensured great work-life balance by encouraging rest. Not only that, the creator loves communicating with His creation, and regularly came down to the garden of Eden to appreciate the atmosphere and relax with Adam and Eve. They discussed many issues at that time, and He still speaks. He communicates through His words, His Spirit, His servants and His creation.

> 'God, who at sundry times and in divers manners spake in time past unto the fathers by the prophets, Hath in these last days spoken unto us by his Son, whom he hath appointed heir of all things, by whom also he made the worlds;'
>
> Hebrews 1:1-2

As we relate to our Father, we should also relate to His son, Jesus Christ. He is our Saviour and the Captain of our souls, who assigns tasks and appraises our performance. He is a God of excellence, therefore he encourages us, and rebukes us for selfishness, laziness and mediocrity. He rebukes us because he believes we can do better, yet He loves us and does not give up on us. Our Saviour is always approachable; He creates time for us and honours our confidentiality. I wonder what life would be like if I called and He was too busy? Thankfully that never happens. What a loving Saviour!

The Holy Spirit is a gentle, powerful and dynamic being. He is very soft-spoken, communicating in diverse ways to gain our attention, and guide us. He operates like dew from heaven, with little fuss and great impact both on a personal and corporate level. He manifests spiritual gifts through believers, and seeks to glorify the Son.

> 'Howbeit when he, the Spirit of truth, is come, He will guide you into all truth: for He shall not speak of himself; but whatsoever He shall hear, that shall he speak: and He will shew you things to come. He shall glorify me: for He shall receive of mine, and shall shew it unto you.'
>
> John 16:13-14

The Holy Spirit is the mystery of Christianity, and yet also the secret of our success. When we submit to His will and authority, the church flourishes. Hence the exponential growth of Charismatic churches all over the world. On the other hand, when church leaders depend on sermons, intelligent analyses and academic achievements based on human wisdom; the church ceases to grow! Why is this?

> 'Which things also we speak, not in the words
> which man's wisdom teacheth, but which the
> Holy Ghost teacheth; comparing spiritual things
> with spiritual. But the natural man receiveth
> not the things of the Spirit of God: for they are
> foolishness unto him: neither can he know them,
> because they are spiritually discerned.'
>
> 1 Corinthians 2:13-14

We are spiritual beings, with a vacuum in our lives, seeking spiritual connection with a divine entity. The spiritual connection can be good or evil. For good connections, His Spirit communicates with the human spirit, and teaches the human spirit, revealing deep spiritual insights as he or she matures in faith. No wonder He said in John 10: 34

Jesus answered them, 'Is it not written in your law, I said, Ye are gods?' We need the nature of our God to operate like gods.

Knowing Jesus

There is nothing as thrilling as knowing our Redeemer. It would be my greatest honour to introduce you to Him. He is the best friend to have. He is dependable, and He will always be there for us. He believes the best of us no matter how many times we fall short of His divine plan for our lives. His aim is to love us, show us the way to the Father, and to offer us the Holy Spirit as a helper here on earth.

> 'That if you shalt confess with thy mouth the
> Lord Jesus, and shalt believe in thine heart that
> God hath raised him from the dead, thou shalt
> be saved. For with the heart man believeth unto

righteousness; and with the mouth confession is made unto salvation.'

Romans 10:9-10

I pray that you encounter Jesus in your life, and believe in your heart that He paid the price of salvation on the Cross. May you experience peace, mercy and joy as you welcome Him in. He has not promised that life will be 'easy' with Him, but that He will be with us through thick and thin. He speaks to us often through scriptures, as we learn to discern His voice in personal and corporate worship. Attending a church in order to grow spiritually, and worship with fellow Christians, also helps.

For some, coming to know Christ is a gradual process, not a single occasion like the one experienced by Paul in the Acts of the Apostles, and that is fine. Whatever the situation, may Christ transform our lives and communities for good.

Life in Christ

People sometimes ask me, 'how come you are happy all the time?' What we focus on, magnifies in our lives, and we will experience what we believe. God is good all the time, irrespective of our circumstances, and His nature does not change. We must seek, and focus on, things that make us happy and keep us youthful.

Finally, brethren, whatsoever things are true, whatsoever things are honest, whatsoever things are just, whatsoever things are pure, whatsoever things are lovely, whatsoever things are of good report; if there be any virtue, and if there be any praise, think on these things. Philippians 4:8

Prayer can therefore be summarised as accessing heavenly resources for earthly use, for all things are possible in Christ.

Questions to ponder

- ❖ Have you encountered disappointments that shook your faith?
- ❖ What can hinder you from pursuing the things of God?
- ❖ How has Christ affected your faith walk?

EPILOGUE

I hope this book has stirred you to pray more. Prayer can be exciting. Prayer changes things. Prayer is speaking to the Almighty in the presence of His angels and the elders in heaven, with Jesus advocating your cause according to the Father's will. Prayer is also about hearing updates from heaven. It can also help us see into the future, as well as responding to the here and now. Prayer strengthens. Prayer stretches. Prayer challenges. Prayer consoles. Prayer grieves. Prayer comforts. Prayer rejoices. Prayer adores. Prayer is about touching heaven and blessing the earth. It impacts the generations to come. Prayer is humanity cooperating with the divine to establish Christ's rule on earth. Like David, let us declare His kindness to us:

> 'And David the king came and sat before the Lord, and said, 'Who am I, O Lord God', and 'what is mine house, that thou hast brought me hitherto?' And yet this was a small thing in thine eyes, O God; for thou hast also spoken of thy servant's house for a great while to come, and hast regarded me according to the estate of a man of high degree, O Lord God. 'What can David speak more to thee for the honour of thy servant?' For thou knowest thy servant. O Lord, for thy servant's sake, and according to thine

own heart, hast thou done all this greatness, in making known all these great things. O Lord, there is none like thee, neither is there any God beside thee, according to all that we have heard with our ears. And what one nation in the earth is like thy people Israel, whom God went to redeem to be His own people, to make thee a name of greatness and terribleness, by driving out nations from before thy people whom thou hast redeemed out of Egypt? For thy people Israel didst thou make thine own people for ever; and thou, Lord; becamest their God. Therefore now, Lord, let the thing that thou hast spoken concerning thy servant and concerning his house be established forever, and do as thou hast said. Let it even be established, that thy name may be magnified forever, saying, the Lord of hosts is the God of Israel, even a God to Israel: and let the house of David thy servant be established before thee. For thou, O my God, hast told thy servant that thou wilt build him a house: therefore thy servant hath found in his heart to pray before thee. And now, Lord, thou art God, and hast promised this goodness unto thy servant: Now therefore let it please thee to bless the house of thy servant, that it may be before thee forever: for thou blessest, O Lord, and it shall be blessed for ever.'

1 Chronicles 17:16-27

Amen.

BIBLIOGRAPHY

1. BAKER, P. (2005). *Secrets of Super Achievers*. Whitaker Inc.
2. CAROTHERS, M.R. (1980). *From Prison to Promise*. Christian Books
3. CHO, D.Y (1979). *The Fourth Dimension*. Seoul Korea. Logos Int.
4. GASS, B. (2011). *The Word for Today*. Stoke-on-Trent. UCB Ltd
5. HYBELS, B (2014). *Simplify*. First edition. GBR. Hodder and Stoughton Ltd
6. MILUM, J. (1893). *Thomas Birch Freeman* – Missionary Pioneer to Ashanti, Dahomey and Egba. NY
7. MURPHY, J (2010). *The Power of Your Subconscious Mind*, NY. Penguin Putmac Inc
8. OYEDEPO, D (2006). *The Wisdom that works*. Second edition. Dominion Publishing House.
9. PRITCHARD, J (2015). How do I pray? Publisher SPCK.
10. The Holy Bible – King James Version (KJV)
11. www.GREATSITE.COM – English Bible history

THIS BOOK WAS
WRITTEN FOR

❖ those interested in spirituality
❖ those seeking to improve their prayer lives
❖ those wishing to lead prayer meetings efficiently
❖ those wishing to experience spiritual gifts
❖ those wishing to discern and fulfil their calling
❖ those wishing to engage in ministries abroad
❖ the discipleship of young Christians.

May you find joy in His presence, Shalom.

Printed in the United States
By Bookmasters